Servant-Institutions in Business

Jerry Glashagel

Servant-Institutions In Business

Published by the Greenleaf Center for Servant Leadership
770 Pawtucket Drive, Westfield, IN 46074
Printed in the United States of America.

Book and cover design by Joe Hunt

SERVANT-INSTITUTIONS IN BUSINESS

JERRY GLASHAGEL

THE GREENLEAF CENTER FOR SERVANT LEADERSHIP

Dedicated to
Dorothy and Bob Glashagel
and their advice:
You can be anything you want to be,
just do a good job of it!

Contents

Introduction

Robert K. Greenleaf launched the modern servant leadership movement with the publication of his first major essay, "The Servant as Leader," in 1970, which focused primarily on the individual servant-leader. His second essay, "The Institution as Servant," published in 1972, focused on institutions and their trustees.

Greenleaf begins "The Institution as Servant" with a paragraph that many people have called "the credo":

> This is my thesis: caring for persons, the more able and the less able serving each other, is the rock upon which a good society is built. Whereas, until recently, caring was largely person to person, now most of it is mediated through institutions–often large, complex, powerful, impersonal; not always competent; sometimes corrupt. If a better society is to be built, one that is more just and more loving, one that provides greater creative opportunity for its people, then the most open course is to raise both the capacity to serve and the very performance as servant of existing major institutions by new regenerative forces operating within them. (1)

What an important statement for today!

Greenleaf knew that institutions have a huge impact on the quality of our lives. He believed that institutions and their leaders should be concerned about everyone they touch—employees, customers, business partners, and the neighborhoods in which they work.

What, then, is a servant-institution? It is an organization that intentionally and effectively serves everyone touched by it. It is led by servant-leaders–persons who serve first, then choose to lead. It trains its managers in servant leadership. It supports the development of every member of its workforce, working to unleash the energy and intelligence of each person. It listens to its customers, and then develops products and services that serve their customers' wants, needs and interests. It works with business partners to create win-win-win relationships—a win for the customer, a win for the business partner, and a win for the organization. Finally, a servant-institution is a good neighbor. It cares about the community and finds ways to partner with others to create a better society.

What do servant-institutions in business look like? That's what this book is about. Each organization is unique in the ways it chooses to serve. Each is in a different business, has a different structure, offers different products and services, and resides in a different community. Yet there are common threads that tie servant-institutions together. They strive to make decisions that will, simultaneously, help both the people they serve and the organization's bottom line. They don't choose between growing the bottom line and growing people—they insist on both. They believe that growing people is the best way to sustain the bottom line. Servant-institutions are committed to the long haul, to steady growth and to results that benefit every one of the stakeholders, rather than any one group over another.

This book is about eight businesses that are in various stages of their growth as servant-institutions. I have had the opportunity to study them, talk with their leaders, and in most cases, visit their workplaces. Not all of these businesses use the words "servant-leader" or "servant-institution," but all of them are applying the principles.

The eight companies are very different from each other. There are small, medium and large companies from different industries. Three are private, closely held corporations, three are employee owned, one is publicly traded, and one is a mutual life insurance company, in effect customer owned. Some have unions, and some do not. Some of the companies have been intentional about servant leadership for several decades, and others started their journey within the past three years. Each is on its own path, learning from its own experience and from the experience of others.

The first eight chapters tell the stories of servant-institutions:

TDIndustries, DuBrook Concrete, First Fruits, SBLI USA Life Insurance, Festival Foods, Johnsonville Sausage, Toro, and PPC. When we survey the members of the Greenleaf Center and query our conference attendees about how we can help them, they often ask for more examples of organizations that are applying the principles and practices of servant leadership. This is a book of business examples. In this mix of stories, you will find ideas that you can adapt and apply to your own situation. Some of these ideas may challenge you to raise the bar for your organization.

While they will never look exactly alike, when we look at a number of different organizations, common threads and shared issues can be seen. The ninth chapter summarizes the characteristics of servant-institutions and their service to each of the four groups of people they touch: employees, customers, business partners and community partners. It also discusses the role of servant-leaders within these companies.

The final chapter is yours to write. The questions for reflection and discussion provide the framework for you to use in thinking about your organization. In what ways is your organization already applying these principles? Where might you focus your energy in order to make your organization more of a servant-institution?

We can learn from the experiences of others. But in the end, it is a matter of what each one of us does, the initiatives we take, the efforts we put into serving everyone our organization touches, and the commitment we make to transforming our organization into a servant-institution that matters. I hope you find this book helpful.

1.

TDIndustries

Some people do leave, but most of them come back

When it comes to employee turnover, TDIndustries doesn't fit the typical construction industry profile. They do everything possible to make TD a company that you join for life. It might sound old fashion–but look at the results.

Founded in 1946, TDIndustries now provides a wide range of facility maintenance and specialty construction for commercial, industrial, and institutional buildings. They specialize in heating, ventilation, air conditioning, piping, plumbing, electrical, high purity piping, building integration and refrigeration systems, and they provide operation, maintenance and repair of those systems. The $300 million company primarily serves the southwestern United States.

By all of the financial measurements, TD is a very successful company in a very competitive, cyclical industry. Their revenue, net income from operations, net worth, and working capital are enviable. They have had no debt in several years. They have weathered many storms—slowdowns and recessions.

What's different about TD is not the products they sell or the services they provide. It's the way their people relate to each other, to their customers, to their business partners and to their community partners. At TD, it is all about people.

Jack Lowe, Sr. discovered Robert K. Greenleaf's essay, "The Servant as Leader," in the early 1970s. He engaged everyone in the company by inviting groups of 20 at a time for an all-day discussion of values. Every three weeks for a year and a half he opened his home to a different group. With the invitation they received a copy of Greenleaf's essay and were told that it would be one of the things they would talk about. When, in the end, servant leadership was adopted as the leadership style for TD, it was not Jack Lowe, Sr.'s decision. It was a decision made by the company. Everyone was involved. Everyone had a say in this company-defining decision.

Today TD is a third generation servant leadership company. Today servant leadership permeates life at TD.

When new employees join TD they become *partners* and *members of the family.* A woman who came to TD as a temp says that on day two she asked the person she was working with: "What's in the air here?" She felt that TD was somehow different from anyplace else she had worked—full-time or as a temporary. This woman is still with TD several years later, no longer a temp. Another TD employee likes to talk about how surprised he was when the CEO called him by his first name the second day on the job!

For many at TD a key to serving employees is the family culture. Listen to what several employees have to say about this:

We want to be the kind of place you're proud to tell your friends and family about. It starts with the respect we have for each other. It's kind of neat to see all the different cultures and backgrounds. I believe it's a real good thing that everybody's on a first-name basis. I know I have three kids myself, and they're always asking, "Dad, when are we going to work with you?" You want to be successful in your business; you want to be successful in your family. We want to be both.

In a TD video that includes brief quotes from a dozen different employees about this special environment and how it has shaped their personal thinking about their career at TD, a woman says:

> I was a high school dropout. I had mentioned that I wanted to get my GED. And my supervisor came to me one day and said, "We want you to do this because it is important to you." And I'm happy to say that I finally passed it, as of this past month.

In the same video a Latina woman shared:

> I had always heard that growth here would happen very quickly. They've taken care of all my trainings throughout the seven years I've been here. I didn't even think I could do it, but my supervisor believed I could.

An African-American male employee shared this insight when discussing how almost everyone makes a lifelong career out of working at TD:

> Every now and again people do leave. But for the most part, the majority of them return, and the reason for that is because they understand that it is a great company to work for, it's a great place to work.(2)

Best places to work

It is not surprising that TD has been on *Fortune* magazine's list of "The 100 Best Companies to Work For in America" every year since the program began in 1998. What is impressive is that TD takes the process a step further. At TD the data collected by the Great Place to Work Institute for *Fortune* magazine ranking is posted on the outer wall of every manager's cubicle.

They don't just bask in their ranking, they manage to the data. TD works with the Great Place to Work Institute to produce data on all employees, not just the sample required for the *Fortune* list. This gives TD management the data for each work-group to see how they are doing each year and where they can improve. TD management looks at credibility, respect, fairness, pride and camaraderie at the work-group level as well as the organization level. Each work-group compares themselves with other units within the company, between this year and the last three or four years, and with other organizations.

Internally, supervisors at TD get additional feedback from the people they serve—their direct reports. A 30-question survey is completed by each person, compiled and used in coaching sessions between the supervisor and her/his supervisor. Here are a few of the statements in the survey questions: *My supervisor ... displays belief that I am an important member of the team; actively guides my training and development; recognizes and builds on my strengths; can be trusted to speak the truth and keep his/her word.* At TD, growing great employees is not an "unfunded mandate." It is a commitment that is measured. It is a commitment for which each manager is held accountable. It is a commitment that employees feel from day one.

At TD, servant leadership has been the hallmark of the company for three generations. It is communicated through the mission statement, company values and leadership style. It is woven into the house rules in meeting rooms, and it is sounded loud and clear through a huge banner in the plant.

Here are examples of how they articulate servant leadership at TD:

Our Mission

We are committed to providing outstanding career opportunities by exceeding our customers' expectations through continuous aggressive improvement.

Leadership

Simply and plainly defined,

- Leaders are people who have followers. They have earned recognition and respect.
- Leaders are first a servant of those they lead. They are a teacher, a source of information and knowledge, and a standard setter, more than a giver of directions or a disciplinarian.
- Leaders see things through the eyes of their followers. They put themselves in others' shoes and help them make their dreams come true.
- Leaders do not say, "Get going." Instead, they say, "Let's go!" and lead the way. They do not walk behind with a whip; they are out in front with a banner.
- Leaders assume that their followers are working with them. They consider others Partners in the work and see to it that they share in the

rewards. They glorify the team spirit!

- Leaders are people builders. They help those around them to grow because the leader realizes that the more strong people an organization has, the stronger it will be.
- Leaders do not hold people down, they lift them up. They reach out their hand to help their followers scale the peaks.
- Leaders have faith in people. They believe in them. They have found that others rise to their high expectations.
- Leaders use their hearts as well as their heads. After they have looked at the facts with their head, they let their heart take a look, too.
- Leaders keep their eyes on high goals. They are self-starters. They create plans and set them in motion. They are persons of thought and persons of action–both dreamers and doers.
- Leaders are faced with many hard decisions, including balancing fairness to an individual with fairness to the group. This sometimes requires a "weeding out" of those in the group who, over a period of time, do not measure up to the group needs of dependability, productivity and safety.
- Leaders have a sense of humor. They are not stuffed shirts. They can laugh at themselves. They have a humble spirit.
- Leaders can be led. They are not interested in having their own way, but in finding the best way. They have an open mind.

Servant leadership at TD is lived in key actions of leadership and management. Everyone works in cubicles, including the top three officers. No executives have a corner office. Rather, the corner rooms are used for team meetings. Even in good years, the total compensation of the CEO is held to a modest 10 to 15 times the total compensation of the average employee.

TD is employee owned. Everyone is served: owners, employees, customers, business partners and community partners. It is a servant-institution, which means that it is focused on the people—all of the people. Results, including financial results, are tied to specific groups of people.

When asked how one would best measure the effects of servant leadership on the business outcomes of a construction company, a sharp, young member of TD's management said: "It's simple. Just look at the safety record and the callback rates of the company."

The result of long-term servant leadership at TD is high quality work. The customer is served best by the company that is servant-led. In turn, the employee owners of the company are served best by the profitable, highly respected, productive company.

Accidents and callbacks cost the company; thus they cost the employee owners. Delays caused by accidents and work that results in callbacks cost customers time and money. Servant leadership focuses on the obvious and the subtle influencers of quality work. Servant leadership focuses on making sure that employees—partners—at all levels are supported, in every way possible, to do the best job they can for the customer and for themselves.

Facing hard times

How has this worked out when times turned tough for construction? The answer is found in the crisis TD faced in 1989. Texas construction dried up between 1984 and 1990. TD found itself with few new contracts in 1989 yet with a lot of unfinished, over-budget projects. Competition was fierce. Their bond company became demanding. Then the bank TD worked with failed.

They needed cash but there were no outside sources available to them. So they turned to the employees. Jack Lowe, Jr. invited everyone with over five years of service to a meeting and laid out the facts. He told them that the defined benefit retirement plan was $1 million overfunded and that the only way to access that was to terminate the plan, and that he recommended doing so. After some discussion, the group agreed. Jack went on to say that the company needed another $1 million to have a chance to survive and the only source available was the $4 million that would be distributed to the participants. They couldn't force anyone to participate but they wanted everyone to have a chance to do so. Then they worked out a formula that would produce $1.5 million if everyone participated. Over the next few weeks, enough employees agreed to invest their retirement funds to the tune of $1.25 million. The employees saved the company. The culture of trust built over the years paid off.

Serving community partners

If you were to check the board rosters of the educational, cultural and social service organizations in Dallas, you would find a very interesting fact. One company has more employees on those rosters than any other–and that company would not be the largest employer in Dallas. It would be TD.

Everyone at TD is encouraged to get involved with both community and professional organizations. And they do. It is an expectation. It is also something that is modeled by the top leaders. Jack Lowe, Jr. has been the elected Chairman of the Dallas School Board for the past six and a half years. Other TD leaders are currently officers of the Community College Board, the Community Foundation Board, and the Chamber of Commerce. A half-dozen different professional societies always have one or more TD employees on their leadership roles, as well.

Jack Lowe, Jr. has an interesting perspective on the value to TD of serving community partners. According to Jack, this is the best leadership training TD leaders can get. Unlike in the corporate world, when trying to lead in a non-profit organization or on a government board, the leader has to be skilled at listening and serving. The followers in these community settings really do have a choice to follow or not. They are also volunteers, not employees. Jack suggests that his servant leadership is really tested when he chairs a school board meeting on a complex, emotional issue. It puts his leadership role at TD in a whole new light!

2.

DuBrook Concrete

Building a better world through worthwhile work

DuBrook Concrete in northern Virginia seeks no less than to have gung-ho employees, raving fan customers and ecstatic suppliers. In what others might view as a simple commodity business, DuBrook stands out. They are in a people business.

DuBrook Concrete's roots go back to 1946 when fighter pilot Jack Ogorchock returned from WWII. He founded a small trucking company to deliver building materials to construction sites. In 1992 three of Jack's kids took over and in 2004 they divided the company based on interests and geography. Tom Ogorchock is the president and owner of DuBrook Concrete, located in Northern Virginia near Washington, DC.

Gung-ho employees

> DuBrook employees drive our business and we place a high value on them having jobs about which they are passionate. We want all of our employees to understand what they do at DuBrook is important, they are making a valuable contribution, and we are committed to each person's growth and development.(3)

With employees from 15 countries and cultures, speaking six different languages, what DuBrook looks for when they hire new employees is the desire to work in a family atmosphere that supports and encourages teamwork. What they find is that regardless of culture, people want to know that their work is worthwhile and that they can be emotionally connected to both the organization they work for and a larger purpose.

For what is known as a high employee turnover business, especially in terms of the largest part of their workforce—the concrete truck driver—DuBrook places a lot of emphasis on training. They want to engage each new employee, helping him or her succeed at DuBrook. They have individual growth and development programs for each employee. They promote from within whenever possible. They do everything they can to let each employee feel valued, appreciated, and needed.

Beginning in 2007, they initiated a training program in servant leadership for all managers and supervisors. *This means [each supervisor] is committed to being a servant first to those employees they manage and supervise, and a leader second. This management style promotes and fosters an environment that is motivating and inspiring, and where people work together to help one another succeed.*(4)

DuBrook managers are always looking for the good in others. They look for simple ways to recognize the hard work of employees. Cheering each other on brings enthusiasm to the workplace. But when celebrating success, the focus is on teamwork—the success of the company and of everyone in it, rather than a focus on the success of top leaders.

> At DuBrook, employees are valued as individuals, encouraged to team, empowered to take ownership of their individual and team responsibilities and, as a result, are accountable for their actions.(5)

Raving fan customers

> Just having satisfied customers is not good enough. We strive for customers who are raving fans—those willing to actively and enthusiastically recommend our products and services to others. (6)

The DuBrook strategy with customers begins by listening to each customer. At one level, all concrete customers want the same thing—the concrete they order, on time! At another level, customers want something different. They want specialty mixes and additives. They want DuBrook to understand the importance of their project. Each customer feels that his or her project is both unique and critical. DuBrook employees listen carefully to the customer on the other end of the phone line or right in front of them. They take the time to let each customer know that they get the message: This project is urgent and demands our undivided attention.

DuBrook knows that customers are well informed. They deserve to be treated with respect. *First we seek to understanh–hen be understood.* Two of the most important reasons that customers become raving fans are, they are listened to with respect, and they receive the unique product and service that they want and need.

In addition, customers want access to every department at DuBrook and they want to be treated the same way throughout. They don't want to get one message from sales and a different message from dispatch. Every project represents a set of experiences for the customer. Every customer represents a whole matrix of relationships from sales to accounting. Making each experience positive is the job of everyone at DuBrook.

Ecstatic suppliers

A concrete business requires thousands of tons of raw materials. DuBrook depends on suppliers to consistently provide quality materials on time. Similarly, they rely on other suppliers for trucks and parts, conveyor systems, maintenance equipment, tools, computers and software. They rely on banks to provide the capital to fund operations.

> Our suppliers are an integral and critical component of our business. In order to meet the demands of our customers, we continuously strive to enlist the products and services of only stable and ethical suppliers who have longstanding reputations in the industries they service. We focus on developing relationships with our suppliers that are based upon trust, mutual respect and an intimate understanding of our respective businesses. (7)

This means working with suppliers as partners. "*We want our suppliers to be just as excited about doing business with us as we are with them. This excitement grows by being partners in mutual progress and growth. It is an excitement that is not based solely on the number of transactions, dollars or cents, but more importantly on an intimate understanding of each other's vision, successes, failures and challenges."*

The common thread in all three areas–gung-ho employees, raving fan customers, ecstatic suppliers–is to be found in the DuBrook slogan: *Building a Better World Through Worthwhile Work.*

Work is worthwhile when everyone is listened to with respect, teamwork is expected, and customer success, supplier success and company success are what's celebrated. At DuBrook they call it a servant leadership environment.

Over the past three years, Tom Ogorchock has had the opportunity to sell DuBrook Concrete to major suppliers. Vertical integration at the national and international level has become the goal of the major cement manufacturers. Tom has made the tough, personal financial decision to stay independent. He is committed to building and maintaining a servant-institution. Selling at this time would most likely be at the expense of servant-institution values for the DuBrook leaders, managers and work force.

For Tom, the DuBrook team is just getting started on a path they would like to see influence their industry even more than consolidation.

Getting started

The DuBrook story is not one of decades or generations of servant leadership. Top leadership at DuBrook formalized their commitment to servant leadership in 2006 by creating a position at the holding company to focus on developing and implementing a comprehensive servant leadership program. They hired Colin Searcy to put it together and supported him with direct access to President and owner Tom Ogorchock and Senior Operations Officer Jack Hartman. Tom and Jack knew that in order to make servant leadership the leadership style of the company, they couldn't just delegate it to Colin. It had to change the way each of them works with everyone, day in and day out.

Colin started by learning all he could about servant leadership from books, conferences and conversations. He laid out a strategy to train managers and supervisors, followed by truck drivers and other front-line workers. He created three training modules. One module introduces servant leadership, links it to the DuBrook vision and core values and beliefs, and highlights the characteristics of servant-leaders. A second module focuses on key attributes of servant-leaders, effective communications of servant-leaders, and overcoming inhibitors to servant leadership. The third module focuses on listening skills, team building, conflict resolution and how servant-leaders deal with difficult people.

Colin teaches each module with a small group of DuBrook employees from different departments and levels. Thus, servant leadership is introduced as a company-wide practice, and each module provides opportunities for diverse staff to experience training together, in a way that shows mutual respect and builds a culture of trust.

After each module there is a test participants take to reinforce what they have learned, and to provide the basis for recognition by the employees and their colleagues that they have taken another step on their servant leadership journey.

Hand in hand with the development of the new training program was the development and implementation of a 360° measurement system and a coaching process, to make servant leadership a part of the expectations for everyone. *What gets measured gets done.*

The measurement system is focused on servant leadership. It does not replace other job performance tools. It is simple yet powerful. Twice a year each manager or supervisor invites his or her own supervisor and direct reports, plus at least two peers to complete a thirteen item Growth Input Form. No punches are pulled. The questionnaire asks in specific ways: How am I doing on the practices of a servant-leader? How can I improve? The Growth Input Forms go to Colin and he compiles them. The person being measured then sits with their supervisor, who shares the responses.

The reason this works at DuBrook is that they have built, and continue to reinforce, a culture of trust. The title of the form is intentional and significant: *Growth* because the growth of each employee is the goal, and *Input* because it is given in the spirit of support for improvement. There is no sense of "gotcha." Everyone has gone through the same modules so those giving feedback know they are part of a system designed to support the whole DuBrook team as they all move in the same direction.

Does that mean that everyone gets it? No. Senior Operations Officer Jack Hartman, for one, will tell you there have been a couple of people who have chosen not to work in this environment and have moved on. That's a part of taking servant leadership out of President Tom Ogorchock's office and into every corner of the organization.

After training all DuBrook managers and supervisors, Colin began training drivers—the front-line workforce. These classes are very "hands on," with lots of individual and group participation. Like the managers and supervisors, drivers respond positively over time as they try different key servant-leader practices on the job and at home. At first there is a combination of positive personal identification with the values and principles, yet reluctance to change behavior in established relationships and routines. *I'd like the world to be like that but I'm not sure it can be.*

Behavior change takes time, and small steps are required. By introducing and teaching servant leadership; by measuring and coaching everyone as they learn to apply servant leadership; and by systematically starting at the top and working all the way throughout the organization and putting resources behind it all, success is possible. The DuBrook leadership is confident it is working for them. They are early in their journey compared to most of the other companies in the stories that follow. But they are moving at a pace that offers hope to any company that is asking, "Where should we start and how long will it take to become a servant-institution?"

3.

First Fruits

A Family Farm

> This really is a family farm, even though it's huge. We see it as a whole bunch of families working together to make it happen. Ralph Broetje

With over 5,000 acres of orchards, close to 2,000 employees, and a packing facility handling an average of 20,000 boxes a day, First Fruits is a big operation. It is not what we usually think of when we hear the phrase "family farm."

But Ralph and Cheryl Broetje are also not the kind of people we usually thinks of as heading one of the world's largest apple producers. Neither Cheryl nor Ralph has a college degree. Their résumé is simply the story of Broetje Orchards from 1968 to today. Their education in management theory has come from reading and discussing the *Bible*. The Broetjes believe faith and business can be incorporated in a single mission.

"Sure, we have to make money or we'd have to shut the doors," Cheryl Broetje explains, "but profit isn't our main motive. It becomes the byproduct of treating people with dignity, respect and mutuality, and as equals in every sense of the word. We all have a role to play in creating a community of people who care for a business that then cares for them. We believe if we ever stopped doing that, we would implode."(8)

Year-round employment

Their approach has had a major impact on First Fruits employees and their families. The tradition among apple growers is to contract migrant labor for short periods of time and keep the corporate payroll at a minimum. The Broetjes saw the negative influences of this system on family life both in the United States and in Mexico. So they made business decisions that were good for employees *and* their business. They found ways to extend their growing season to bring fresh fruit to market for a longer period through the year, thereby enabling employees to work year-around.

Ralph is highly skilled at introducing new apple varietals, which open new markets while also creating the need for more all-season jobs. He keeps as many employees as possible moving from crop to crop within their operation, both picking and pruning. The Broetjes expanded into packing to control more of the process; to create more year-round jobs for employees; and to provide job opportunities for more members of the family. The packing plant employs wives of pickers and pruners. The family is supported and spouse-employees are more stable, and feel more useful, productive and successful.

Today First Fruits has 1,000 permanent employees, plus another 900 seasonal laborers. This is a huge shift from the industry norm, which would typically be 400 year-round employees and 1,500 seasonal laborers.

Development of affordable childcare

Along with the shift to permanent employment came the need for affordable childcare. One year after the packing line was opened, a daycare facility, New Horizon, was built on-site to help working parents feel more comfortable at work, and at the same time provide more jobs for additional family members. Today this is not primarily about babysitting, but rather about preparing children to enter kindergarten on a par with other students.

A second goal of New Horizon Center is to develop the academic and leadership skills of staff. All 23 of their staff—from custodians, to teachers, to office staff—have been working to advance their own education, including GEDs, CDAs (child development associate degrees) and English proficiency. They do this during evenings and on weekends—to improve themselves and to be better role models for the families they serve.

Development of safe, affordable housing

Continuing to listen to their employees, the next need they heard loud and clear was that of safe, affordable housing; many were living in overcrowded, dilapidated structures, surrounded by gang activity. So they invested profits from the business in the construction of on-site housing. Vista Hermosa, the small community they created, became home to 650 people.

As a part of this project, they built a gym and chapel to be the focus of the residents. They wanted to be certain that it would never be called a labor camp, but instead a community.

A board of directors, made up entirely of residents, was formed to oversee the association. This provides an important leadership training experience for the board members. They set the rental rates and determine what programming is provided to families from soccer to folklorico dance, parenting and health classes, financial planning, youth groups, summer youth leadership and college prep programs.

Two additional housing initiatives have recently been launched: one to provide seasonal housing on-site and the other to offer affordable homes for purchase by lower-income families. The seasonal housing includes 108 beds in 18 new townhomes. The area with affordable housing is called Tierra Vida. Habitat for Humanity and Hayden Homes are partners in this multicultural development. The Center for Sharing, their first non-profit venture started in 1986, is now located in a building in Tierra Vida called the Collegium, complete with a coffee shop, computer lab, and public meeting spaces.

Investment in youth through relationship-building and scholarships

As the Broetjes became more involved with families at Vista Hermosa, the needs of older youth became clear. In response they created Jubilee

Youth Ranch, a residential program for 50 struggling teenage boys, and they established a scholarship program to encourage first-generation college students who might otherwise not be able to continue their education and pursue their dreams for the future.

Jubilee Youth Ranch provides a one-year program for boys who need to escape their current environment, catch up on academics, rebuild familial relationships, and find a new beginning for their lives.

One program offers scholarships to any child of a Broetje Orchards employee or graduate of Jubilee Academy. They also offer continuing education scholarships to Vista Hermosa employees to constantly encourage them to improve their skills and talents.

Through the scholarship program, they learned that the greatest obstacle for first-generation college students is cultural: the college campus is intimidating and the application process is unknown. Parents with an average 6th grade education are unable to help. With the help of the federally funded GEARUP program they have created a unique college-prep program. It provides mentoring and tutoring to youth and hosts a range of tours to museums, college campuses and other sites to inspire youth and their parents and prepare them for a successful transition to college life. As a side note, the director is a young man who grew up in the community and participated in the scholarship program himself—a true testament to what can be done.

The mission of the K-6 school in Vista Hermosa is to provide "a Christ-centered, world-class education with a commitment to preparing children of diverse backgrounds for success as young scholars, community leaders, and citizens in the world."(9) The staff caters to children of multiple learning and language levels, enabling them to progress at their individual speed and ability. Emphasis is placed on small class size and team-based teaching. To ensure academic success and achievement, extended day and year-round learning opportunities are integral components of the school calendar. Programs include Reading First, 'Meet the Masters' Art Curriculum, on-site Public Library, character education, free food program, Music Program, daily after-school program, and an eight-week 'Camp Vista' summer program. "It has been so amazing to see the changes in the parents and kids," says Ralph. "They become very self-motivated. Although most have little education, they believe they can do anything."

An important element of all of these community investments is that another 150 people are employed to run these operations—the housing, childcare, education and social service projects.

For the Broetjes, servant leadership means that their business goals are not separate from their spiritual values. They are in the business of serving their employees, with whom they are in the orchard business. They make decisions based on what will benefit employees *and* the business. This family farm is indeed a large group of families working together to make it work for everyone involved.

"There's a relationship," Cheryl explains. "We care for the land. The land cares for us. And we care for each other. There is love in the organization. It is about caring. People are the fruit that will last, so our orchards must bear fruit so we can bear fruit that will last."

Servant leadership throughout the company

As First Fruits has matured, servant leadership has become something taught to everyone. Men in the fields have taken servant leadership training. The warehouse manager provides regular courses on servant leadership. The senior management team is constantly studying servant leadership to clarify how the mission and values of First Fruits affects day-to-day activities throughout the company.

For the first time, in March 2009, they pulled all 1000 employees together for servant leadership training and celebration. That meant shutting down the orchard, the warehouse and the community programs to assure everyone could focus on what makes First Fruits very special. Six employees shared what it means to be a servant-leader. Cheryl spoke. Then everyone worked together in small groups to explore how they could grow servant leadership. They have truly reached the tipping point in a unique way.

Community Profit: A Global Concern

> The dream was that I would own an apple orchard and use the money we made to help feed kids in India. Ralph Broetje

As Cheryl tells it: "My husband, Ralph, and I met in traffic court when we were teenagers. He was charged with going too slow in a red Corvette, and I was charged with going too fast in my parents' white Ford station wagon. We thought we might provide a little balance for each other! But he surprised me with his dream to run an orchard a few months after we were married."

Cheryl and Ralph learned from key adults in their lives the importance of a commitment to serve others with a special eye to the vulnerable. They lived with models that empowered others, shared resources with others, and always showed respect for others. They grew up with a strong sense of community and with an appreciation for how important it is to build community in every aspect of life.

As the Broetjes developed their business, they lived these values in relationship to their employees. But early on they reached out beyond their employees to the neighborhood in which the company operated. What they found was that for them, an orchard located in the state of Washington, the neighborhood was global.

In 1982 they took a family Christmas trip to Mexico to learn more about the communities and conditions so many of their employees came from. On that trip they witnessed, for the first time, lives of extreme poverty. They found people living in garbage dumps, cardboard boxes and pitiful one-room homes literally piled on top of each other.

On that trip Cheryl had a life-changing experience. She recalls:

> Our family was volunteering with an organization that works along the Mexican border. We arrived at a home just as a mother came out and said the baby next door had just died. She put a bowl of rice in

> our hands and asked us if we could please feed her child (while she consoled the bereaving mother).
>
> We went in to find a young adult woman with no ears or eyes tied on a box waiting to eat. My friend began feeding her, and I sat by her side putting my hand on her shoulder. Then this young woman began to feel my face. Soon she seemed to lose interest in the food, and instead, gave me a hug and then lay on my shoulder. This small incident changed my life. I realized in that moment that all persons have gifts to give—she gave me her attention, presence and love. And those gifts strengthened my life; they lit up a dark corner in my life. We realized that our Latino farm workers all had gifts to give that, if called out and received, could strengthen us all. Even the work of running a business was no longer to be a unilateral plan by owners alone, but one of many diverse people coming around a common mission and becoming community in the process.(10)

With a better understanding of "how hard it was for people there to dream about achieving anything, because the opportunities did not exist," Ralph said, "I understood that (our employees) were coming to the United States for better opportunities for their families. It gave us more insight into what their needs are, and it reminded me of why we had this orchard."

After building homes and apartments for their own employees, the Broetjes decided to reach out to migrant labor communities in Latin America, and then Africa and Asia. They listen and find projects where they can contribute.

"Broetje Orchards is committed to caring for those who work in our business and for those in need around the world. Each year we donate about 75 percent of our profits to local, domestic, and international projects. We believe that this moral foundation is the primary reason for our company's business success."

Seventy-five percent of the profits? What does this mean for a successful agri-business? How does this work for a very busy, working couple that has nine children, ages 23-40, six of whom are East Indian by birth, and nine more grandchildren? It means they serve the global community with heart, soul and profits.

Broetje Orchards use two vehicles to serve their global neighbors. The first is Vista Hermosa Foundation, which currently seeks (1) to build partnerships with organizations working in Kenya, Uganda, Tanzania, India, Mexico, Central America, Haiti, the Dominican Republic and the USA; and (2) to fund faith-based, community-oriented initiatives focused on one of three areas of development: hunger alleviation and economic empowerment, education and leadership development, and immigration in the USA.

The second vehicle is Cherry Donations, an effort that takes 100 percent of the profits from the sale of cherries (the original 50-acre orchard where the Broetjes started) and entrusts employee committees to make donations to non-profit organizations of their choosing.

For the Broetje family members and employees who guide and operate the foundation, hunger alleviation and economic empowerment today means supporting food security and self-sufficiency, micro-enterprise development, agricultural training and development, women's empowerment, health and nutrition, and freeing individuals from exploitative work conditions. Education and leadership development means supporting women, youth and their communities through access to formal and non-formal education, vocational training, and servant leadership development. Immigration in the USA means building relationships with faith-based partners serving immigrants and advocating for positive policy reform.

These grant-making guidelines translate into specific projects that serve the global neighborhood in which Broetje Orchards lives. A sample of recent grants includes a servant leadership house for young adults in Mexico; a five-week seminar in servant leadership, held in Africa, for clergy from Kenya, Uganda and Tanzania; and support for organizations working on these issues:

- Housing and community development in Haiti and the Dominican Republic

- Sustainable agricultural training in Marimanti, Kenya
- Eradication of forced prostitution in Jamaica and India
- Women's micro-enterprise development in Mexico
- Creating a just market for small farmers in Chihuahua, Mexico
- Eradication of child labor through education in Andhra Pradesh, India
- Education and leadership development of Maasai girls in Kenya

Cheryl Broetje considers this the "community profit" side of the business. It is not an afterthought or a luxury or an option. It is a part of the original dream—an orchard that would help feed kids in India.

4.

SBLI USA Mutual Life Insurance

Rooted in a deep belief in human potential

There was a time in the past when Americans held their financial institutions in high regard. They trusted the person they dealt with at the company and they trusted the company.

SBLI USA Mutual Life Insurance Company, Inc. is an insurance company that still enjoys a 97.1 percent customer satisfaction rating. That's because they work hard to earn it every day. Their mission statement reads:

> We help individuals, families and communities access information and products to achieve financial goals. Our focus is service, affordability, preservation, and growth of policyholder value. Our business philosophy blends financial strength and innovation. We are rooted in a deep belief in human potential.

Vikki Pryor, President and CEO, likes to talk about things like their ranking on *Crain's New York Business* Best Places to Work in New York City; being named Underwriter of Choice by the United States Hispanic Chamber of Commerce; SBLI USA's new Women's micro site dedicated entirely to the interests and financial planning needs of women; having Customer Centers not only in New York City but also in Buffalo, New York; Chicago, Illinois; Glendale, California; and Bayamón, Puerto Rico; and their social responsibility record of supporting more than 50 different community and cultural initiatives over the past seven years, through company and employee efforts. Although SBLI USA doesn't call it servant leadership, they are committed to and organized around serving employees, customers and communities.

SBLI USA was founded in 1939 as the Savings Banks Life Insurance Fund through the vision of former U.S. Supreme Court Justice Louis Brandeis. Its products were marketed by representatives at participating "community savings" banks in New York, influenced by Brandeis' belief that ordinary working people should have access to affordable, quality life insurance. In the 1990s, 16 separate affiliated insurance departments of issuing banks became a single mutual company and was renamed SBLI USA Mutual Life Insurance Company, Inc. Since then they have expanded nationally, including Puerto Rico. Today SBLI USA, together with its subsidiaries, has $1.5 billion in assets, $15.8 billion of insurance in force, $127 million in surplus capital and $170 million in annual revenue.

For SBLI USA, service comes naturally, from their roots. Building on and maintaining that culture in the fast-paced financial sector over the past decade makes their story important. They have made tough decisions to keep serving their target market as they have expanded. Their focus has always been on working families, in what is referred to as the middle market (households with annual income of $25,000 to $99,000) who are generally overlooked by other financial services providers. But SBLI USA has not turned its back on these folks as it has grown and expanded across the country. For example, its presence in Puerto Rico to engage the diverse, working community there is unique.

Making business decisions and balancing and meeting the needs of the people they serve and the products they can offer has not been easy. The challenge has been in meeting the evolving needs of the market in a highly-regulated business with many financial pressures.

Vikki Pryor had to work long and hard to lay out a viable plan to focus on working families, many of whom are single parent families. The conventional wisdom was that the target market of SBLI USA was not wealthy enough for the Company to approach. Pryor and her team were undeterred. She held out for the principles SBLI USA was founded on—the principles they had succeeded with in the past and which they saw as critical to their mission for the future. Pryor contended that SBLI USA would succeed precisely because it would serve its employees, customers and communities, and that all three would be in a very real sense one and the same.

Let's take a look at each of these three groups of people SBLI USA touches: employees, customers, and communities. What does serving each group mean at SBLI USA?

Employees

SBLI USA talks *careers* rather than jobs. *Start your Life Insurance Career with SBLI USA – The Best Place to Work.* They look for *talented individuals* for important positions. They offer a thoughtful and fair benefits package and a significant number of company-sponsored programs and services for their *associates.* SBLI USA is committed to ensuring that all associates *at all levels* have access to an array of services and programs that *help them balance their work and personal lives.* Notice the tone of this: careers, talented individuals, programs and services for all associates, commitment to helping balance work and personal lives.

The benefits are people-centered and include retirement savings in the form of a 401(k) with a company match, and after five years a pension plan kicks in. They offer medical, dental, and vision insurance and FSAs (flexible spending accounts). Education and growth benefits include tuition reimbursement for pursuit of undergraduate and advanced degrees, as well as extensive in-house training programs including a fast-track management program and an extensive list of industry-specific continuing education courses and certifications. In terms of personal needs, SBLI USA offers transit programs, domestic partner benefits, and an Employee Assistance Program where associates and their families can receive professional, confidential counseling and referral services to help manage personal, family, and other problems of daily life.

SBLI USA employees mirror the diversity of the target market of their customers. Employees speak 20 languages. Two-thirds are multicultural. A total of 57 percent are women.

In recognizing SBLI USA as one of the 50 Best Places to Work in New York City, *Crain's New York Business* quoted SBLI USA employees:

- "We have a strong commitment to promoting from within, and our people move around a lot within the company because they want to and because they are encouraged to learn and move up," says Michael Akker, COO.
- "Once people ask for an opportunity and think they can do it, they will eventually be given that job," says Mr. Anthony, who started as a staff member in finance nine years ago and moved up to Director of Finance himself.
- "The people I work with are very nice, my superiors are very considerate and if you need to talk to management, the doors are open," says Amilbia Aguedelo, a sales and service representative at the company's walk-in customer service center in Manhattan.

In initiating Crain's Best Places to Work list in 2008, Steven Blader of New York University's Stern School of Business helped frame the issues of great workplaces this way: "People are seeking more than just a job. All of these companies are validating people and making them feel respected." Blader went on to say, "All (of the) perks may not survive the recession, but companies that have a culture of respect will be better able to navigate the difficult waters ahead. Being honest with employees, involving them in decisions and acknowledging the painful repercussions of cuts are essential." SBLI USA is a model of what Blader is talking about.

Customers

Serving employees models how SBLI USA expects employees to serve customers.

SBLI USA customers are diverse, working Americans, including women. They reach customers through unique, innovative insurance stores and engaging websites created by monitoring their customers and responding to what they need.

Take the store in Bayamon, Puerto Rico. It is located in the Walmart wing of the Plaza del Sol Mall on Main Street. There are kiosks where customers can quickly and simply take financial self-assessment quizzes, learn about SBLI USA products and services, and obtain insurance quotes. This is fun stuff for what might otherwise be a very intimidating experience.

The SBLI USA store in Buffalo, New York is similarly located in the Galleria Mall and has the same interactive kiosks. This store also has play areas with games and plasma TVs to occupy the kids when parents move from the kiosks to conversations with customer service personnel.

Online SBLI USA services its customers 24 hours a day, 7 days a week. They have a web community that engages their customers. Customers not only talk with SBLI USA online, they are able to engage themselves in a number of self-educating, self-servicing tools to manage their accounts.

Many customers come to SBLI USA through the website using tools such as *Plan Your Life, the Insurance Calculator, Glossary of Terms* and the online options it provides. SBLI USA is committed to its mission to help individuals, families and communities access information and products to achieve financial goals. Through its online presence the company offers educational web features: financial tools, calculators, product information, seminars, downloadable forms, pay online and manage your account. The community shares real life stories. Working families in 49 states are buying life insurance and annuities on the SBLI USA site. Their customers do not all live within walking distance of the SBLI USA stores, but they can all connect through the web.

The SBLI USA site and the call centers are completely bilingual—English and Spanish. Each kiosk, web-based and phone-based tool, program, product or service is as comfortable for their Spanish-speaking customers as their English-speaking customers. The United States Hispanic Chamber of Commerce (USHCC) has formed a key alliance with SBLI USA offering its members all of the SBLI USA products—employee group life insurance as well as individual life insurance and annuities. Small businesses can connect with SBLI USA through either the USHCC website or the SBLI USA site. Through this partnership SBLI USA reaches even more working families that are often at the lower half of the middle market, a segment that is generally overlooked by the insurance industry (households with an annual income of $25,000 to $50,000).

The commitment of SBLI USA to effectively use technology in serving their customers is cutting-edge, not only for financial services; but especially for connecting with their target market. They have received high recognition from CISCO for the way they are using technology to reach, engage, sell and service customers. Technology is making a difference in what SBLI USA stores look like, in how they reach women, Hispanics, small businesses, individuals and families across the country, and the way customers are in control of their own financial education, planning, purchasing, and managing of their accounts. Technology has changed the speed of information flowing back and forth between the organization, employees and customers. With the information SBLI USA gains from their web community they can quickly develop new products and services for their steadily growing customer base.

Community

The definition of community has changed for SBLI USA over the years. It has changed geographically from New York alone to 49 states, as well as the District of Columbia, the U.S. Virgin Islands, and Puerto Rico. It has evolved from those who came into physical contact with each other each day in the neighborhoods of the banks and offices where the insurance was sold, to now include those who connect through the web but have never met each other in person.

What hasn't changed is the commitment of SBLI USA to a sense of community…individuals living in families, people helping each other, depending on each other and caring about each other. President and CEO Vikki Pryor puts it this way: "We see our customers as people with whom we can develop long and productive relationships. That's why we also have a vested interest in seeing the communities we live and work in thrive. We know this is an integral part of making us prosperous as individuals and families."

SBLI USA reaches out to communities in specific ways. The company encourages employees to spend time in the neighborhood with paid personal commitment days, during which they are encouraged to volunteer, and to join others in working with non-profit organizations that benefit everyone. The company has participated in events like Earth Day, and the Walk for Breast Cancer. Over the past seven years they have also raised more than $750,000 in support of over 50 different community and cultural initiatives.

It is the synergy of company, employees and customers that is so impressive about how SBLI USA serves the community. The company's decisions about community engagement are made with a single criterion: Will the effort serve the community *and* our customers in that community, using our financial resources *and* our employees' time and talents, and will the effort contribute to the security of the community?

More formally the SBLI USA Social Responsibility Statement puts it this way: "SBLI USA strives to be a leader in the empowerment of people and communities and the preservation of a just and sustainable society."(11)

5.

Festival Foods

Great stuff for not a lotta money

Paul and Jane Skogen got started in the grocery business in 1946 in Onalaska, Wisconsin. Their single store joined the Independent Grocers Association (IGA) in the '50s. They were an important part of their community back when local businesses were where people did all their shopping. People counted on the Skogens for good meat, seasonal fruit and vegetables and all their staples. It was where many kids got their first job. These characteristics were influential in developing the Skogens' family store into the community business people counted on.

When Paul died in 1976, Dave and Barb Skogen took over along with Dave's two brothers. Eventually, Dave and Barb's kids, Mark and Sue, joined them and the four Skogens own the business today. By 1990, they had expanded to five stores locally, and joined the Festival Foods concept. Today, they have expanded with 13 Festival Foods stores across Wisconsin, averaging over 75,000 square feet each and employing over 3,200 full- and part-time associates.

Much has changed since it all started in 1946. Some would argue that the customer has changed the most. Customers have a lot more choices as to where and how they buy groceries. They have new ideas and expectations about products and services. They live faster-paced, more complex family lives. They have more demands placed on them, so they generally demand more of the organizations they deal with on a regular basis.

Serving customers and communities

The Skogens have responded with an impressive list of innovations within their Festival Foods stores. Each store has eight to ten different departments: Bakery, Meat, Produce, Natural Foods, Deli, Seafood, Signature Items and Organics. They feel more like a food mall than an old-fashioned grocery store. They also have an extensive breakfast, lunch, and dinner catering operation. Most of their stores have Tot Spot childcare areas for kids 18 months to seven years of age, staffed from 9:00 a.m. to 8:00 p.m. daily. This means busy parents can concentrate on grocery shopping, focus on the many choices and decisions they have in the store, and get their shopping done more efficiently. This is just one example of how Festival aims to have their guests leaving feeling better than when they arrived.

But innovation really comes to the fore when one looks at all Festival Foods offers customers online: a recipe center provides a huge library of information and some very helpful tools, such as: a recipe of the day, meal planner, My Recipe Box, Top 50 recipes, and quick and advanced search tools where you can look at all of these variables at once. You can search for what course you want a recipe for, the total preparation time it will take, the required skill level, the region the recipe comes from, recipes appropriate for specific holidays, and the equipment you will need to prepare the recipe.

Then there is the "ask the chef" feature that allows customers to ask questions about anything related to cooking—how to prepare, measure, slice and dice, cook or store, and a million other concerns the diverse customer population can think of. There are cooking videos that can be watched on demand, online, 24/7. You can go to "Nutrition support," where customers ask Lisa the nutrition consultant any question they may have. She responds in less than 24 hours with a nutritional analysis of specific foods, nutrition information related to heart disease or diabetes or weight management, as well as nutritional meal planning advice.

Or, you can go shopping online, selecting the groceries you need from a comprehensive, easy-to-use list. You can also find the weekly newspaper ads, coupons, and sale items posted on their website. Their site is interactive, allowing one to use the monthly planning tools, including the Deli Department's Hot Bar calendar, which lists what fresh items are going to be offered six weeks out. Then there is Upromise, a program customers can join that places 5 percent of the purchase price of selected items into a college savings account each time they shop at Festival Foods or other participating stores.

Some things do not change

If they were alive today, Paul and Jane Skogen probably would not recognize their grocery store in Onalaska or the other 12 stores Dave, Barb, and Mark operate in Green Bay, Manitowoc, Oshkosh, Appleton, Fond du Lac, De Pere, Holmen, Marshfield, La Crosse or Eau Claire. They probably would not understand how the web works. Needless to say, a lot of things have changed since 1946.

One thing has not changed: customers still want the store to serve as their agent for price, service and quality! Paul and Jane would be proud of the way the Skogen core values have remained unchanged. The mission of Skogens' Festival Foods is to develop a team of associates dedicated to providing customers with a clean store, friendly people, quality products and an enjoyable experience "for not a lotta money."(12)

The innovations listed above certainly indicate that the Skogens are staying in tune with their customers, providing quality products and an enjoyable experience.

One of the most important keys to the Skogens' success in sustaining a people-centered, culture-driven company is that the Skogens are hands-on leaders. Each of them can be found on the floor in one of their stores, almost every day of the week. They know how to cut meat, stock shelves, prepare baked goods, run a cash register and bag an order. And they know how to do it with a smile and a friendly comment to the customer or associate.

Here's a measure of how effective they are at modeling their values: We asked community leaders in Manitowoc, Fond du Lac and Marshfield about the role of Festival Foods in the civic life of their town. In each case, the local leaders talked as if the Skogens lived in their area, not 150 to 200 miles away in Onalaska. Everyone we asked knew Dave or Mark Skogen. Most had heard Dave tell the Festival Foods story at a service club or Chamber of Commerce meeting. The Skogens seem to be hands-on in 13 different places at the same time.

It's not just the Skogens who are tuned into customers (officially called *guests* at Festival Foods). All employees are trained, motivated, supported and accountable for building relationships with guests. Priority number one at all times is serving the customer. Ask any employee a question and they'll stop what they are doing and talk with you. The associates are taught that they are in the relationship business; they happen to sell food.

Guided by servant-leaders, Festival Foods is a servant-institution in terms of serving their customers and their communities.

Currently (2009) the Skogens are concerned about the depth of the economic recession. But notice their focus: *How can we listen even better and with more care to what our customers are worrying about? How can we respond even faster to their concerns?* Servant-institution behaviors in hard times don't really change. Rather, they intensify. What works in good times also works in bad times.

Serving employees

It's difficult to sustain customer service unless an organization serves its employees first. Festival Foods gets it. Dave says that a mission statement should tell you how a company plans to work and succeed in the field it is in. That is what Festival Foods' mission statement reveals, and it is not only found in annual reports and on a web page. At their annual company-wide *Festival College,* all 200+ managers have been known to recite the mission statement together with enthusiasm!

There is a level of energy in the *Festival College* that reflects the depth of the service culture. Messages are broadcast about positive relationships and growth. Relationships win customers and produce profits; and profits are plowed back to support growth. Practicing this knowledge has allowed them to make statements such as: "We've doubled revenues in the last five years with an average annual growth rate of 20 percent." It is exciting to see how this growth equals opportunities for existing and new associates.

As the CFO and COO take the platform it becomes clear that they enjoy providing leadership at Festival Foods. They are having fun. They brag about performance, share the credit with everyone in the room, and weave together numbers and relationships. They emphasize the importance of everyone's leadership. They focus on comments such as, "Be strong and clear on values. Balance finance, operations and people. Lead by example, starting with supporting every associate."

At the *Festival College* the room is filled with men and women in their twenties and thirties. They all seem to know each other. They work on store teams, market teams and department teams. It is a genuinely friendly group of people.

One measure of how deep this culture is can be found in the fact that all 13 stores are operating full tilt while all of these leaders are off at the college for three days. And to prove it the CFO and COO start the day with sales figures for each store for the day before. The figures for almost all of the stores are ahead of the forecasts for those specific days.

In one of the workshops at the college the subject is 'employee benefits.' Sure, Festival Foods has a solid set of benefits but what they discuss in this workshop is not the specifics of health care or paid vacation or retirement programs. What they talk about is the concept of the company being the most important benefit. Working for Festival Foods is a benefit. Employees feel important and appreciated. The benefits of products and programs come and go. Relationships last. Relationships can be built and maintained by managers committed to doing so.

Two needs are universal: the need for meaningful relationships and the need for meaningful work. The goal of Festival Foods is to provide employees with both.

Servant leadership at Festival Foods is talked about, clearly articulated and regularly celebrated. It is not subtle. It is right up front. Everyone feels it and that feeling is contagious.

6.

Johnsonville Sausage

Why work for Johnsonville?

Johnsonville Sausage, headquartered in Sheboygan Falls, Wisconsin, is one of the largest producers of bratwurst, breakfast sausage and Italian sausage in the U.S. Johnsonville products are sold through retail grocery stores, restaurants and fast food chains as well as directly to families via their website. Their products are available in 27 countries in North America, Europe and Asia, including China and Russia.

At over $400 million in annual sales they are a significant family owned business with an impressive, consistent annual growth rate over the past 10 years. Once a regional Midwest company, they are now an international leader in the meat products manufacturing and distribution sector.

But why work for Johnsonville?

You might be a brat-lover who lives in Wisconsin, or a member of the Stayer family whose father or grandfather founded the company in 1945. You might have a strong background in food science or manufacturing, sales or distribution, or be a trained chef or former restaurant owner. There are places for the right person who has any of these reasons to want to work for Johnsonville. But these good reasons cannot account for more than a small percentage of the 1400 people who have chosen to work for Johnsonville in North America or Europe.

The reasons people work for Johnsonville are more to be found in the way employees are treated, regardless of their position in the company, rather than in their past training or qualifications. Johnsonville is a unique place to work because of its approach to employee empowerment.

Everyone at Johnsonville is called a *member* rather than an employee. Every member has a personal growth plan. Members are expected to be engaged in lifelong learning. They are supported when they choose to seek a new challenge within the company. And they are challenged to provide stellar performance every day.

The roots of all this can be found in what they call *The Johnsonville Way.*

> "We at Johnsonville have a moral responsibility to become the Best Company in the World. We will do this as each one of us becomes better than anyone else at defining, and then serving, the best interest of all those who have a stake in our success.
>
> We will succeed by setting near-term objectives and long-term goals that will require personal growth and superlative performance by each of us. We will change any objectives or goals that no longer require personal growth and superlative performance to ones that do.
>
> As an individual, I understand the Johnsonville Way is about my performance and my accountability to the team. My commitment to stretch, grow and excel is an unending one. This is the Johnsonville Way and I am committed to it."(13)

Each new Johnsonville Member is introduced to this statement when they join the team. Then they begin to learn what it means.

Showing up and doing the things in the job description are not enough. At Johnsonville it doesn't work that way. It is the member and the supervisor working together, setting long-term goals and short-term objectives, that defines the job. Over 400 of Johnsonville's members defining what they want the world to become for them feels very different.

Each of these members develops two or three long-term goals. At Johnsonville they take a good deal of time defining each goal not just through a typical, short statement but also in terms of how they will know when the goal is realized. The first time a member goes through this process it might take a couple of months.

Once a member delineates his or her goals, the focus shifts to hammering out shorter-term action steps and measurement processes. It is a disciplined program that sets Johnsonville apart.

Continuous learning

Continuous learning is another part of the Johnsonville Way. By supporting members with learning opportunities, the members grow and the Johnsonville products improve. Here is how they define continuous learning to prospective and new employees:

> When you focus on Member Development, you do the following:
>
> - You understand your strengths and weaknesses.
> - You put yourself in situations where you can learn new things.
> - You take an interest in the world around you.
> - You learn from your mistakes.
> - You read or take formal classes when you need to.
> - You meet people who work at other companies and learn from them.
> - You ask others for feedback and use their advice.
> - You write and follow through on a development plan each year.
> - You use what you learn.
> - You do whatever it takes to help others develop their skills.
>
> The word "you" stands out here. That is because it is up to you to learn and grow. Others can help, but nobody can do it for you.(14)

Team Work

Teamwork is probably the oldest component of the Johnsonville Way, having been the driving force behind the first revolution of the way in the 1980s. Here is how they talk about teamwork with prospective and new employees:

> Teams defined, and implemented the Johnsonville Way. Some may

remember pride teams, spirit teams and great performance teams. While the teams took many forms, they all took ownership for excellence in their areas of expertise. This was more than simply delegating tasks. Teams defined strategies, plans and budgets to help Johnsonville become the "Best Sausage Company in the World." By working as a team and balancing the knowledge and skills of all the team members, performance and results have been greater than any one individual could have accomplished.(15)

Who is our customer?

In the late 1990s, a shift in thinking at Johnsonville involved realizing that the *consumer* is not their *customer*. The customer is the person who buys from Johnsonville and sells to someone else. The brat lover is the consumer. The store or restaurant owner is Johnsonville's customer.

The job of everyone at Johnsonville is to serve the customers in ways that result in the success of that customer. The goal is to create win-win results. It doesn't matter if you keep the floor clean or align the labels correctly, or if you are the CEO or the training manager. What you do must serve the customer by helping the customer succeed. A clean floor is related to a safe brat. The alignment of the label demonstrates attention to detail and speeds up the check-out line at the grocery store. Every little detail of what is done at Johnsonville is connected to a detail of the customer's business.

One of the critical ways Johnsonville employees serve their customers is by being very good listeners. An example of extraordinary listening to customers is when one Johnsonville team spent a week in their customer's world. They worked alongside this particular customer to solve a problem that they first had to understand by being there. Instead of sending a single troubleshooter, a team was sent and worked out a solution that they then used to improve things back home. It was listening and teamwork at its best.

Organization as servant

The family members who own Johnsonville are Ralph C. Stayer and Launa R. Stayer-Maloney. Ralph became president in 1978 when their parents turned over the reins to the next generation. He attributes the success of the company over the past three decades to their approach to empowering employees.

Ralph teamed up with James Belasco to write a book on empowering employees: *Flight of the Buffalo: Soaring to Excellence, Learning to Let Employees Lead* and Tom Peters included Johnsonville Sausage in his pivotal book: *In Search of Excellence: Lessons from America's Best-Run Companies.*

Launa Stayer-Maloney was instrumental in expanding sales, building a national and international sales force and growing the company from the marketing side. Today she represents the community service dimension of the family and the community by playing key leadership roles with the Sheboygan County Development Board, Mount Mary College (Milwaukee), and the Boy's and Girl's Club Foundation.

The Stayers don't call themselves servant-leaders. But a couple of their managers responsible for organizational development and learning suggest that in the case of Johnsonville Sausage, the organization itself is the servant. This is an insightful way of expressing what we mean by a servant-institution. The Johnsonville Way, not just as a mission or vision statement, but rather as a living entity, guides the organization in becoming the servant of the employees, customers, business partners and community partners. In Ralph Stayer's words: "Most companies use their people to build a business. At Johnsonville, we use a business to build our people."

7.

The Toro Company

Seed, Not Sod

Ken Melrose began a 36-year career at The Toro Company in 1970. From 1983 to 2006, Ken as president, then chairman of the board, worked to make Toro a servant-institution. But the transition started out rough, very rough.

Toro was financially down and nearly out in 1981. In the late 70's the company was on a roll. In 1978-79 they doubled sales and tripled earnings over the previous year. But in 1980 and 1981, everything went wrong—product quality, sales direction and volume, and overhead costs. The company lost $13 million in 1981 when sales plummeted 50 percent below the previous year. In 1980, the CEO fired some of the key executives, and by the end of the year he decided to leave Toro too. Shortly thereafter the banks cancelled Toro's credit and Wall Street wrote them off.

At that point the board asked Ken to lead a turnaround and rebuilding effort. Together Ken and the board essentially said: "Let's take a deep breath, start over and build a company that will last." Their strategy might not turn things around quickly, but they felt it would be better to make Toro a solid, trustworthy company that people would want to work for, businesses would want to partner with, and customers would want to buy from. In landscaping terms, they chose to seed, not sod.

Ground rules for growth

Here are the ground rules for growth, as explained by CEO Ken Melrose, in his book *Making the Grass Greener*:

1. *Seed Not Sod*—In a culture that's accustomed to quick results, seed not sod isn't an easy choice. Seeding takes time and quite a bit of care. Eventually, however, it results in a healthy and more resistant turf.

2. *The Team Comes First*—This concept can be hard to accept initially because there is a bit of the maverick in most of us. We have a high propensity to honor individual heroes. We think differently, however, when we consider the masses of technicians, engineers, and unnamed individuals who stand with (each hero) and make their accomplishments possible.

3. *Provide Guidelines and Support*—Before you will see much growth, you have to provide people with guidance and support, especially if the concept of teamwork is new to them. Like the old horse that pulled the milk wagon a few generations ago, your team may only know the one way of working—and the fault is no one's but your own.

4. *Close the Perception Gap*—One exercise I use with my managers points out the gap between management's and employees' view of what creates job satisfaction. Managers are asked to rank ten job satisfaction factors from the employee's point of view. Later I reveal a comparison of how a group of managers thought employees would rank these factors to how the employees themselves ranked them. The two lists indicate a significant management perception gap. I believe these misconceptions exist largely because we're locked into old ideas and norms. We all have concepts of what the words management and labor mean. For the twenty-first century, more accurate and more positive terms would be team leaders and team members.

5. *Select Team Members*—We incorporate three basic premises in the selection method we use at Toro: 1) each one of us has great potential, 2) potential is best achieved when people are allowed to perform, and 3) the best performance comes from people who are inspired, motivated, and encouraged; committed to a vision, goal or task; empowered to execute their vision; and recognized for their part in completing the vision.

6. *Empower the Team Leaders and Members*—Once the team is selected,

empower the team by clarifying expectations, goals, schedules, parameters, roles, responsibilities, consequences, and guidelines. Empower team members by allowing them self-direction and freedom to fail(with learning). A leader's role is to create an environment where people can achieve their potential as they move toward their goals.

7. *Kill the Seeds of Discontent*—Often skepticism and cynicism fester within the supervisory ranks. This can be very confusing to employees: to hear one set of values and have quite another imposed within their work environment. This incongruence sows the seeds of discontent. To avoid such diseases, you must either sharpen the blade or replace it.

8. *Do Unto Others*—Toro's long-term financial goal is to be a company that can demonstrate consistent revenue growth and earnings performance in the face of our inherent seasonal and cyclical vulnerabilities. We build a platform from which to pursue this goal by being trustworthy and valuing associates and our team members. That leads to a more productive contributing organization. Then when everyone is directed to satisfy customer requirements (inside customers as well as outside customers), market leadership becomes more likely. Market leadership in turn enables consistent and sustainable growth in earnings, a target that attracts and holds shareholders.(16)

A company people want to work for

Over the next two decades, Toro became a company people wanted to work for. They focused a great deal of energy on learning about their people. They studied and experimented with the concepts of empowerment, trust, teamwork, recognition, shared rewards, open communication, celebration, honesty and integrity.

Ken personally embraced the idea that employees should be treated as whole persons. He invited groups of new employees to his office for coffee or lunch each month. He didn't talk at them in those sessions. Rather, he asked them questions about themselves, their families, and their interests. He listened to them and got to know them.

The company began to value the experience, skills and perspectives of every employee. They created a management-plant participation program. All company officers were asked to work much of a day on the assembly line. Officers can learn a lot by walking in the shoes of the people on the front line. The first time they did this, one group of executives worked the entire day on the lawn mower assembly line. By the end of the day they were still struggling to make 80 percent of the line rates. And quality control was right there to correct any mistakes before the mowers went into the cartons. The plant employees had a great time showing them that they really did know how to do things the managers couldn't do. The execs learned that the ability of their plant employees to build mowers both quickly and accurately was far superior to their own. It became clear who should be making the decisions regarding lawn mower assembly.

There is also a job-switching program at Toro. This helps employees within the plant appreciate each other, build their confidence, and prepare for change. Here's an example in the words of Toro employee Karen Bradford:

> Have you heard the expression, "Don't criticize until you've walked a mile in the person's shoes"? Some Toro employees discovered what it's like to work in another area of the Irrigation Division's plant when a couple of departments started exchanging two employees at a time to experience job demands on the opposite side of their own work cells. Juana Alvarez, a general assembler, and Lucy Juarez, a molding machine operator, were among the first. Before working on the molding machine, Juana wondered why some parts kept coming back with defects. Lucy would say, "There's a lot of pressure in molding. We're expected to do a lot, and we try very hard." Juana learned that most problems are not the operator's fault, that the machines cause difficulties. Lucy said, "We get frustrated when we don't send good parts to the line." Juana could see that the operators wanted to do their best, but they needed more help with the machines from technicians. Lucy concluded: "Everyone should try exchanging jobs. We try very hard to send parts right. We don't want to see the part back again! We want to send it out perfect. Let's catch the problem here before it goes to assembly. We care about the product."(17)

At Toro they invest in helping every employee grow and develop both personally and professionally. Employee Anne Waldherr gives us an example of what this means:

> I started at Toro in February of 1991 as an administrative assistant. Although I enjoyed secretarial work, I knew I had more to offer this company in another capacity. The policy of Toro to post openings internally is the reason I am where I am today (1995).
>
> I went after a job titled associate merchandising representative, and due to Mr. Scott Barlass, director of Consumer Marketing, I was promoted to the Marketing Department in January of 1993. Scott told me later that he saw something in me and my abilities that he felt would make a contribution to his team. Because I was allowed to bloom and grow, I feel my contributions to Toro will grow as well. When I was given the job in marketing, I was encouraged to pursue the college degree that I left unfinished in 1980.
>
> If more companies encouraged their employees to strive for excellence and achieve their highest potential, they'd be much more successful.(18)

Teamwork is another critical concern at Toro. It is one of the best ways to empower people with different skills and talents, while stretching them to grow and appreciate each other. Teams are where corporate culture is felt and tested.

Greg Kliner, operations at Toro Irrigation Division, tells a story about teamwork and developing employees under stress:

> When I returned to Toro after a five-year absence, it was like working for a different company. Now there is pride in accomplishment, concern for the employee, an emphasis on teamwork, consistent direction from the upper management, and genuine concern for each employee. Decision-making has been decentralized; meaning leaders no longer dictate the methods for achieving results. When team members devise their own methods and are successful, the leader

> shares the victory. We have an inverted pyramid—the leader serves the people by removing barriers and mentoring.
>
> For example, when it was decided that we would move from a volume-oriented manufacturing process that lacked proper focus on customers, quality, and cost, to a process that was customer focused and quality driven, many people thought it was foolishness. I heard all of the reasons why it wouldn't succeed. Our management team, however, supported me. Our sense of passion to make a difference was renewed and was supported from the highest levels. I found that the greatest tool I had to work with was the positive attitude of my staff and our hourly employees, who also believed they could make a difference and be a part of the solution.
>
> The real test came the day it was announced that we were going to absorb manufacturing, engineering, and scheduling into work teams. This plan involved the dissolution of two departments. The announcement rolled through the division like thunder. This was our first step in flattening the organization. I wanted to put the resources where they could have the most impact—in the day-to-day manufacturing operations. When we rolled out these new processes, they were not instant successes. In the first two weeks productivity dropped, rejection rates went up, and every alarm bell in the division went off. But then we were right back on track after two weeks and we never looked back. We were given the freedom to fail, were supported in our risk taking, and were encouraged to give away power to the functional areas within the organization.(19)

As the new culture developed at Toro, it became a company people wanted to work for because they felt good about themselves and their contribution, about their co-workers and about the products they produced together.

A company others want to do business with

Toro also became a company others want to do business with. Take the credit situation the company faced in 1983. They needed to find a new group of banks willing to extend a $140 million line of credit. They had three years of weak numbers. So they built their case not on past performance but on their plans for and approach to the future. They talked with the banks about long-term, slow growth. They talked about Honda, their new competition, and how Honda, like other Japanese firms, had 50-year plans. If Toro was to compete, they needed to build a company that knew how and why they would be around far into the future, not how they would beat out a short-view American firm the next quarter.

Three banks agreed. They appreciated the Toro values and the new management team. The banks partnered with Toro, taking risks with them, because they believed in the same vision for the future.

Distributors are one of the main business partners Toro has today. The network of independent distributors had been turned off in the late 1970s when the previous Toro management began to focus on the big box stores that insisted on buying direct. The new management returned to a strong, long-term commitment to independent distributors. They listened to their distributor-partners, working with them on new product ideas and discussing what the end customer wants and needs. They grew together. What was good for Toro was good for the distributors and vice-versa.

In 1989 Toro wanted to buy Cushman-Ryan, the maker of turf utility vehicles. They saw it as a perfect addition to their steadily growing relationship with golf courses, where they sold irrigation equipment, turf growing and mowing products. The Cushman-Ryan vehicles would be synergistic. They needed $18 million in equity capital to do the deal but had only half that available. So they tested their trust relationship with their distributors. At a meeting they asked if any distributors wanted to invest in the Cushman-Ryan deal with them. They gave them a day to sign commitments—clearly not enough time to do normal due diligence. The response was overwhelming. The next day the distributors gave Toro commitments for $11 million. The deal did not go through, but both sides of the business partnership learned that they trusted each other and they shared common goals.

A company customers want to buy from

Toro became the manufacturer of choice for a wide variety of customers—golf course managers, landscape contractors and homeowners, alike. Serving customers is a cornerstone of servant-institutions. Toro is a good example.

Serving customers is about many different things, listening to them, responding with new products, offering new solutions to their problems, and staying in constant communication with them. When customers give you feedback, positive or negative, you listen. The positive feedback tells you what to continue doing right. The negative tells you what to change.

Those at Toro who work with the golf course market like to tell the story of Don Clemens, a good customer. Don was hired as the superintendent of the new Blackwolf Run course in Kohler, Wisconsin. When he arrived, the watering system was about to be put in. When he found out whose system it was, he insisted that it be returned and that a Toro system be purchased. They did, it was installed, and the course opened to high reviews and rankings by the likes of *Golf Digest*.

Two years later at a Wisconsin meeting of 80 of Don's peers, he was a speaker. His comments included:

> I hope that when making buying decisions, you all understand the importance of supporting the Toros of the world—the companies that spend money on research and development—not the 'me-toos'... If you don't support the Toros of the world, they won't have the money, or they won't be here to spend the money, for research and development to further improve equipment to allow us to maintain our golf courses.(20)

Like many manufacturers, Toro has layers of customers. There are golf course managers who rely on Toro for irrigation equipment, mowers, and dozens of other turf maintenance supplies, tools and equipment. There are the landscape gardeners and landscape management contractors. In addition, Toro has millions of homeowners who are customers. Toro is much more than lawn mowers and snow throwers, because their customers want and need more. Toro sells golf course maintenance equipment, irrigation systems, probiotic fertilizers, municipal tub grinders, moisture sensors, homeowner composters, turf aerators, landscape accent lighting, and lake aerifiers.

What ties all of these customers and products together? Ken Melrose's response is that they all "in some way, preserve or enhance the outdoor environment. We have consciously changed our purpose from providing lawn care maintenance products to *keeping the world's outdoor green spaces beautiful and healthy*… "

By listening and serving—seeding, not sodding—Toro has become a people-centered corporation with a purpose. And they have a culture that supports their pursuit of that purpose.

8.

PPC Partners

We have no sales force

PPC Partners, Inc. is a holding company that owns a series of electrical service and construction firms. Richard R. (Dick) Pieper, Sr., the chairman, joined Pieper Electric as president in 1960. He has spent 50 years applying servant leadership principles to the operation of the company, which has grown dramatically from a small family firm to one of the top electrical contracting firms in the United States, with subsidiaries in the Midwest and South.

Danny R. Buck, president and CEO of Metro Power, Inc., one of the PPC companies in Georgia, describes their business this way:

> Our business is total relationships. That's what our business is. People are the only thing that's any different between our competitors and us.
>
> We try to treat our employees like we treat our customers. That's the ultimate. We treat our employees fairly, they treat the customers fairly, and our customers treat us fairly. So it's a full circle. But if you break any of those links, it would all fall apart.
>
> That's why we have no sales force. Everyone who works here is a salesman based on the quality job that we produce. And we're very competitive. We take the relationships to a higher level of accountability than most companies. We bring something above and beyond just the price.(21)

Dick Pieper will confirm it. None of the PPC companies have sales departments. They have no purchasing agents. They have no chief financial officers. They have no vice presidents of any administration functions. They do not advertise.

Instead, each company is a set of teams all accountable for work that customers pay for. The group includes 14 different companies in electrical construction and service, line construction, mechanical, electrical, machinery rigging and installation, plant maintenance, plumbing and heating, and organic waste management solutions. They have union and merit shops. They are successful in urban rust belt settings as well as southern rural settings.

All of the PPC companies work on the same principal as the original electrical business started in 1947 by Dick's father, Julius Pieper. That premise is explained here, again by Danny Buck:

> Everything we do is not like a normal electrical contractor. We don't cut corners; we don't sacrifice the job for profit. That's short-term. We are profitable, but it is a by-product of doing everything else correctly. Everything we do is building for long-term. Even if it costs us money on the job to produce the quality, we get it back ten-fold.
>
> We want the customer satisfied. It's a moral obligation to provide that kind of quality. Our name is on it. So it's like a piece of artwork to us, if you will. We get the same satisfaction from seeing the finished product as a painter or photographer would get when people admire their work.(22)

Discipline and rigor

PPC is one of the most disciplined organizations you can imagine. They are decentralized, yet they have tight accountability. Peter Drucker, called the greatest expert on management, described PPC's strategy as homeostatic control. If the work is not correct, the person doing the work has the authority to make it right. Each team and ultimately each person is accountable. You know where you stand when you work for a PPC company. Yet you are enabled by having what you need to do the job, to complete the task, and to satisfy the customer.

There are three metrics each company and the holding company look at continuously: 1) safety, 2) customer satisfaction, and 3) employee satisfaction. These three are supported with 30 qualitative and 27 quantitative measures.

Safety is expressed in hours worked without an OSHA recorded accident. It is a common industry standard. At PPC this number has gone up almost every year. And the year after any exception, the following year has gone up over the year before the slip. The line from 1995 to 2007 goes from 20 to 85 hours. This is 275 percent above the industry average.

Customer satisfaction is on a 10-point scale with 1 being low satisfaction and 10, high satisfaction. This run chart is impressive, not so much for the increase it shows from 8.6 in 1995 to 9.0 in 2007, but because it is consistently very high.

Similarly employee satisfaction on a 100 point scale has moved from 82 in 1995 to 86 in 2007. This is a very impressive increase. One hundred percent employee satisfaction will never be possible.

At PPC they go a step further than asking the standard employee satisfaction questions. They ask: *Do employees and the company treat you as you would like to be treated?* This Golden Rule scale was introduced in 2001 and has been between 90 and 94 on a scale of 1 to 100 every year.

Net profit is another measure that they look at but they do not manage to it. They consider net profit a by-product of the other three measurements. Whenever they have focused on profit rather than people, they have slipped. Fortunately they have learned this lesson from experience, shifted their focus back to safety, and employee and customer satisfaction, and as a result the value of their stock has doubled every four to six years.

At PPC Companies, all employees participate in the same benefits and pay program from the top executive to each and every semi-skilled hourly employee. In management there is a totally transparent system of ten levels: L1 & L2 – Lead Person; L3- Fore Person; L4 – General Fore Person; L5 –

Area Fore Person; L6 – Supervisor; L7 – Manager; L8 – Director; L9 – Vice President; L10 – President, COO and CEO. Each level has a published learning program. Every employee can decide where they want to go, look at the published path that leads there, and go to work getting there.

Relentless listening and feedback loops

Listening is highly valued at PPC. Take employee surveys. Each survey is distributed, then results—what they employees are saying—are reported back to all employees. As soon as decisions are made on any and all suggestions, those decisions are reported back to everyone. Then the next piece of the feedback loop is a report on the progress that has been made on implementation.

Another piece of listening to employees is the PPC discipline of post-meeting evaluations. At the end of every meeting of every team on every issue, each participant completes a meeting evaluation. These are tallied and the results are shared. The next meeting had better be better!

Customer surveys are important. Each customer is asked (after each job) to rate the person or department that did the work, in nine areas related to timeliness, quality, response, and value. These surveys are the subject of immediate review. This is information on the job for which a specific employee or team is responsible. It is their job to correct any problems both with the customer and the team. Each listening event starts a feedback loop. They feed back what they heard. Then they feed back what they plan to do about it. Finally they feed back what was done about it.

For departments like accounting and personnel, employees are their customers. They survey their internal customers just as other units survey outside customers.

PPC has an active learning environment. They have courses offered by employees on any subject anyone will teach. It works like this: everyone is invited to describe a course they want to teach, schedule it, and teach it. These are small group classes. Most are for employees, but if the teachers want to, they can invite employees to bring family members, or a course could be for employees of PPC and a business partner of PPC. Each class has an evaluation process that asks participants about the class, providing valuable feedback that is used to improve the class next time. At PPC employees are accountable for both teaching and learning. That's *all* employees.

Listening and feedback loops support each of these corporate premises expressed by Richard Pieper, Chairman:

- We hold the individual in the highest esteem.
- They in turn respect each other and the customer, resulting in caring for all parties.
- Accountability for one's actions is powerful.
- At some time we all will need help, and we will give it.
- To make this work we must continually listen and seek understanding.

Community support

PPC sets aside 10 percent of before-tax earnings to give back to the communities in which they work. In 2008 the PPC Foundation donated to 211 nonprofits in Wisconsin and 169 in Georgia.

The mission statement of the foundation:

> PPC Foundation will pass back to the community, as allowed by each Company policy, prosperity received through its Companies. It will support any operating needs of programs that are available to the entire population.
>
> It is our intention to positively respond to each request from a valid organization, to encourage the quest of those providing the services to make this a better neighborhood, community and world. In this learning process, what the giver experiences in their service to the community may ultimately be more valuable than the services rendered.

Preference is given to organizations in which PPC employees are leading or assuming responsibilities. Consistent with all of the other policies and practices described above, serving the community is everyone's responsibility at PPC, and is meaningful to the extent that employees, not the company, drive it.

The PPC culture

In December 2008, a random sample of PPC employees was asked questions about the corporate culture for a video. The employees who were interviewed ranged in age from 20 to 60, and included white, Hispanic, African-American, female, male, union, and merit shop. Here are some of the things that were said by the men and women in the field:

- The sense of community and family we have at work ties right into the sense of family I have at home.
- Everyday life is affected, such as family safety at home. Things you normally wouldn't pay much attention to now come more to the forefront.
- PPC is very family oriented. Working here has helped me to develop as a person at home, not only as a manager with the company.
- My senior year of college I took a trip to Guatemala to build a bridge, and the company fully funded my trip.
- I was off sick and the company made sure I got paid and looked after me.
- I was surprised by the level of trust given to me right away. You are new to the company, and you get this message, "come and be a part of this really important effort."
- They taught me how to project myself, be more confident around people and out in the field, and what my best qualities are.
- We are allowed to try. Sometimes you have to fail to know what you've done wrong and how you can do it better. We are allowed that freedom.
- Teach younger people to be supervisors and then you can work for them. It's an accomplishment for me to see that the young people reached that point.
- I'm able to tell my children that it's not about the money or the company. It's about helping people. The company has helped me to do that.

These testimonials of employees suggest that the early commitment of Dick Pieper to shape Pieper Electric around high moral and ethical values paid off. The consistent day-in and day-out decisions of each team at each PPC company continue to pay off. Becoming a servant-institution is not easy. It is a journey, a way of living on the part of the servant-leaders throughout the company. Sustaining a servant-institution from generation to generation may be even harder. PPC today is proof that it can be done.

9.

The Characteristics of Servant-Institutions in Business

While the eight companies described in this book have their differences, they also provide vivid examples of the traits that servant-institutions have in common. The purpose of this chapter is to sketch out those common characteristics.

Employees

Serving employees is a good place for servant-leaders to begin their journey toward creating and maintaining a servant-institution.

Each servant-institution is unique. But as we've listened to different servant-leaders, we've heard them generally talking about these three ways they develop employees: (1) Training and continuing education programs; (2) individualized growth and development systems; and (3) advancement and promotion opportunities. The specific training programs, growth systems and advancement policies of servant-institutions are important, but what makes them effective is that the company is continually striving to build and maintain a culture of trust. The culture of trust undergirds the various employee service programs, policies and procedures.

One of the things we learned by listening to servant-institutions—to leaders, managers and members of the workforce—was that the way new employees are treated *from day one* makes a great deal of difference. In most organizations, candidates are recruited because they have impressed the people involved in making the hiring decision. "We would like you to join us because we believe you will be a great addition to our team." Why then do so many companies put those same people on probation the day they start working for the company?

Servant-institutions are different. Some have gone so far as to make all new employees eligible for all benefits immediately—no waiting periods. This type of corporate policy makes a very strong statement about the commitment of the organization to the employee.

Organizations with a deep-seated culture of trust treat each new employee with high respect in a variety of formal and informal ways. They welcome new employees by communicating the assumption that the new employee will be with the company for a long, long time. Repeatedly in our interviews at established servant-institutions, staff at all levels said: "This place *felt different* when I first walked in. It is like no other place I've worked before."

One of those differences is that other employees—supervisors, peers, even top management—take the time to get to know the new employee as a whole person, not just a worker. They share informally and exchange information about family, hobbies, and other interests. They communicate the idea that they care about this new person with whom they will be sharing a great deal of time for years to come.

Equally important is taking time to establish teamwork right from the beginning. New employees are introduced to their specific job and how it relates to the jobs of those around them. New employees get comfortable with policies, procedures, practices and expectations. They learn the rules of the game so they can be effective players. They are introduced to the style of problem solving in the organization. They get a sense of where they fit and how important they are to the success of the organization.

A fundamental component of serving employees is training and education. In a servant-institution everyone is included, not just rising stars. Every job is considered important enough that the company wants everyone to be the best in their field, continual improvement means ongoing training in job skills and continuing education credits.

Even more important in a servant-institution is the idea that training and education are focused on the preparation of the employees for their next jobs, not just for their current jobs. Thus there is an individualized growth and development system, with each employee supported by his or her supervisor, and the organization. The individualized growth plan might be to complete a level of formal education (GED, AA, bachelor or master degree), or it might be to prepare for a very different job in the company or to move up to a supervisory position. The workforce readily talks about how they have been supported in their personal growth and development since joining the company.

One indicator of the organization's commitment to the development of its employees is a low employee turnover rate. Another indicator is the organization's practices regarding promotion. Many servant-institutions have formal policies related to advancement and promotion. They look first to their workforce, and only if they clearly have no one to fill a vacancy do they turn to the outside. Other organizations may accomplish the same thing informally. What a difference this makes in the enthusiasm of employees and the quality of their work! By working for a servant-institution they have an opportunity to become all they can be without changing companies, moving, or starting over. They can invest themselves in their work and find meaning in it. They can discover the advantages of a long-term relationship with colleagues and take pride in their company, what it does, and how it does it.

Because they develop each individual, servant-institutions are good at unleashing the energy and intelligence of their employees. There are several ways this is done: (1) pushing decision-making and problem-solving out to the edge; (2) using teams to develop new products and services; (3) dealing positively with failure that may happen in the midst of risk-taking; and (4) putting the spotlight on creative new ways of working.

One of the biggest barriers to unleashing the energy and intelligence of employees is sending a message to them that they are not authorized to make decisions. They are told to follow the book. They learn to pass the question or the questioner up the chain of command.

Servant-institutions strive for the opposite. Employees who are supported in making decisions generally make great decisions. As Howard Behar, former Starbucks executive suggests: "The person who sweeps the floor should choose the broom."(23) That person is in the best position to know what kind of broom will work best. If employees know what the mission and vision of the organization is, and if employees are provided the best available training in both technical and people topics, then why hold them back from doing the best job they can possibly do? Give them what they need to make good decisions and to solve problems, and then turn them loose.

At the same time, servant-institutions make good use of teams. Small groups of employees can often come up with the most appropriate new products and services. Teams generally mix people from different job functions with different perspectives and with different sources of information. It is in this creative mix that each employee can use his or her individual energy and intelligence. It is in teams that the outcome is often greater than the sum of the parts. Harness the energy and intelligence of employees by using teams.

In an environment where decision-making is pushed to the edge and teams are used to create new products and services, there will be disappointments. Ask people to take a risk and you have to be open to both success and failure. The creative team that boldly tries and fails is the team to which the next challenge should be given. They need the positive support of top management precisely when they fail.

In order to make serving employees a part of the corporate culture, most servant-institutions also invest in training all of their leaders, managers, and in many cases their entire workforce in servant leadership. Part of Robert K. Greenleaf's test of the servant-leader is that those served are more likely to become servants themselves. The focus of this training is generally on understanding the principles and practices of servant leadership, adopting the attitudes of servant-leaders, and becoming proficient at the skills and key practices of servant-leaders. Effective development of servant-leaders in companies incorporates (1) training and testing; (2) measurement and feedback; and (3) coaching and support.

For example, Colin Searcy at DuBrook Concrete put together three learning modules that he teaches to small groups of managers and supervisors. Each participant must pass a test at the end of each module. Then every six months each supervisor invites all direct reports plus a couple of the supervisor's peers to complete a survey on how the supervisor is doing as a servant-leader. These surveys are compiled by Colin, and the input is given to the supervisor's supervisor. Then the two sit down and discuss the results and set goals for improvement. Training, testing, measuring, coaching and supporting each supervisor is part of their personal journey in servant leadership.

Customers

Customers have a great deal of power in the corporate equation. Yet many companies spend little time in any kind of meaningful dialogue with their customers. They let their customers be the silent party that determines how well their company will do this quarter, this year, and this decade. Taking customers for granted is a big mistake.

The first step in serving customers is simply listening to them. Servant-institutions listen to customers all the time. It is a core task. What you learned from your customers yesterday is important, but not nearly as important as what you'll learn by listening to them today. Make plans based on your cumulative knowledge of your customers, but take action based on what the customer standing in front of you is saying right now.

Servant-institutions listen to customers at both the macro level and the micro level. At the macro level, listening can take the form of focus groups or surveys of potential customers. Customer trends identified by outside experts can be a way of listening at the macro level. Daily interactions with customers before, during, and after the sale are the most effective way to listen on the micro level.

As far as the customer is concerned, the person he or she is talking with is the company. That person either listens to the customer, or not. That person either makes the company relevant to the concerns of the customer, or not. That person either communicates to the customer that the company exists to serve the customer, or not.

Effective listening to customers requires a complete communication loop. It starts generally with a question rather than an answer. For example, when an employee asks "How are you doing this morning?" he or she is ideally listening to what the customer says, how the customer says it, how the customer looks, and what the customer's eyes and mouth are communicating. Then the employee's next question asks for more information based on what the employee heard the customer say. Finally, the employee's response should reflect what the employee heard and let the customer know that he or she has been understood.

When Pieper Electric leaders engage the project manager, architect, engineer, or other tradesmen at a construction site in conversations, they start with listening to each individual and to the specific context of the conversation. They reflect and let others know they've been heard. Then they close the loop by taking action and communicating that action to the other people involved.

Customers of servant-institutions generally describe their relationship with the company with terms like: "they listen," "they make things right," "they get it." Remember the young employee of TDIndustries who said that a good measure of a servant-institution would be "the number of callbacks on a project. If the customer is served, there will be no callbacks. The job will have been done right the first time and both parties will know it."

The servant-institution approaches customers with respect. The assumption is that customers are smart and competent. The goal is to engage well-informed, repeat customers in respectful relationships. When customers are treated with respect, employees generally learn very useful things from their customers. When customers suggest ways to improve processes, products and services, it happens in no small part because the employee expects it. If you think customers are beneath you, you will not be able to hear their good ideas. On the other hand, if you think of your customers as experts at using your products or services, you will be much more able to hear their suggestions as to how you can improve them.

At a Festival Foods store, a customer shared a story that says a lot about respecting customers. The very first time this customer shopped at Festival Foods she got home and discovered that the contents of one package was not what the label said on it. She called the store to let them know and the person who answered the phone very simply insisted on bringing the right item to the woman at her home within the hour. The customer was not only highly impressed with the level of service but she was even more pleased by the assumption that she—the customer—was an important, honest and worthy person being treated with respect from the very beginning.

Servant-institutions serve customers by creating products and services that serve their wants and needs. Some companies make products that they hope customers will want. Servant-institutions on the other hand are in such continuous communication with customers that they know their products and services *are* what their customers want and need—or they are in the process of making changes so that their products and services *will be* what their customers want and need. Servant-institutions are engaged with their customers. They are on a journey together.

The sales goal of most servant-institutions is a steadily increasing number of repeat customers. Some call it increasing customer share rather than market share—selling more products to each customer, rather than just acquiring more customers. To do this, servant-institutions find ways to involve customers in new product development. They continually seek input from customers on new product features. They ask their customers how they can improve service. They share ideas with customers and get customer reaction as they try new things. It is all about the customer. Listening to the customer. Treating the customer with respect. Creating products and services that meet the customer's needs.

Business partners

Listening to suppliers is difficult when you operate on adversarial assumptions. There's not much incentive to believe a person you don't think is telling the truth. When there is no mutual trust, why listen? So you go out to bid for every part or tool or service you need every time you need it. Then set up rigid quality control at your end to test every item to the specs you wrote. Control everybody and everything. In this all too common scenario, you are the only person you can really trust.

What a contrast this is with the kind of relationships that are fostered between a servant-institution and its business partners! The assumption made in the servant-institution culture is that it takes a lot of different parties for any one to succeed—we are interdependent. We are all in this together, so let's build a set of relationships that are win-win-win. In each case the goal is for the customer to win and each of the business partners to win.

Every organization has suppliers of raw materials or parts, tools, supplies, talent or intellectual property. Each organization counts on legal, accounting and other professional services, comprising a complex set of business-to-business relationships—relationships that the servant-institution looks at as business partnerships. The continual engagement of business partners is at the core of success for the servant-institution.

Successful businesses of every type invest in listening. Their leaders and managers are good listeners. They take the time to get to know their business partners. They share what they know about the end customer, what each has learned from listening to customers. They continually improve the end product or service by working together.

Business partners get to know each other's business well enough to be able to appreciate what the opportunities and barriers are to each other's success. They do so because they know that the big gains come when they both succeed. They listen to each other out of mutual concern. That's why Johnsonville employees go to work for short periods at the workplaces of their customers. This gives them a much better understanding of their customers' businesses, and how Johnsonville can meet their needs. TDIndustries invites its business partners to join their classes on servant leadership, to help their partners understand how and why TDI does business the way it does.

Business partners treat each other with respect. They don't try to do each other's job. But they want to work well together, and that means knowing a lot about each other. If a problem comes up, the servant-institution has the kind of working relationship with the supplier that allows them to get to the bottom of the issue and solve the problem. That is really only possible within the context of mutual respect. Solving problems together is almost always faster and less expensive than the alternative world of control in which you blame the other party, threaten them, fine them, or attempt to publicly embarrass them.

When business partnerships go well there can be significant payoffs for both sides. For example, Toro has made a long-term commitment to its distributors. They listen to each other, share ideas that help each other. In a very real sense they have built their respective businesses together. Toro resisted every temptation to adopt an alternative distribution system that would put this network of independent distributors at risk. In turn the distributors have done a great job of selling Toro products.

Remember the story of Toro's opportunity to buy Cushman-Ryan, the leader in turf utility vehicles for the golf course market? Toro needed to make an $18 million capital investment to complete the deal. Banks wouldn't give it to them so they turned to their distributors and, pushing the envelope, asked them if they would put up half the money. Based on the culture of trust that existed between Toro and their business partners, within two days distributors had signed pledges for $11 million dollars. Serving business partners can mean surprising things for servant-institutions.

The Toro example is not so uncommon as it might sound. Respectful working relationships are almost always productive business relationships. People want to work together. People want to see each other succeed.

What often gets in the way is a system of barriers—procedures that may have been created when trust was violated, but are applied as if everyone is to be distrusted. Servant-institutions on the other hand are led by people who keep their positive human values up front. They focus a good deal of their time and energy on managing their corporate culture. Their messages to employees and customers and business partners are consistently constructive and positive. The results of this investment in culture are that everyone benefits.

Community Partners

In addition to employees, customers and business partners, servant-institutions touch one more group of people—the community in which the organization exists. There are many different ways of describing this community. Some define this group of people they touch as the immediate neighborhood around the physical plant of the company. Others see their community as encompassing all of the family, friends, and neighbors of all of their employees, all of their customers and all of their business partners. Their community is larger but still defined by their human contacts. A few servant-institutions focus on a community defined by affinity—anyone in a similar situation to that of the employee or customer focus of the organization. A new dimension to the definition of community touched by an organization today is the environmental impact of a company which can be literally global.

Regardless of how a servant-institution defines the community in which they operate, the way they serve the community almost always involves listening to the different voices in that community, identifying potential community partners, treating each partner with respect, investing in the partnership, and making it as productive a partnership as possible.

Servant-institutions listen for a variety of reasons. They want to know what the issues are. They are interested in the needs and wants of their neighbors. They listen to learn who the players are. They seek to assess what organizations they share values with, and who they might partner with in order to have the greatest positive influence. And finally, servant-institutions listen to learn how they are viewed by others. What do they need to do to eliminate any negative impact they have on the lives of others in the community?

Since listening is an established habit of servant-leaders—they listen to employees, customers and business partners—they become natural listeners in the community. This is often a welcome surprise to community partners. It is an asset that a servant-institution brings to a community partnership—careful, respectful listening to diverse perspectives and opinions. Listening is a powerful tool in community collaboration where too often every party leads with prescriptions for and demands of the other parties. Jack Lowe, Sr., who founded TDIndustries in 1946, was known in Dallas as an excellent listener who could bring diverse, even antagonistic, members of the community together to achieve common goals.

A servant-institution enters the community arena not only with their ears open but also with the assumption that every individual and each organization is worthy of their respect. Finding common agendas for improving life for all is shared work. It is easiest done when respect is a shared value. It provides a basis for working together and a motivation to find common cause.

When servant-institutions assess their own strengths and weaknesses related to a community issue, and learn about the individual and organizational community leaders related to that issue, they will often form a partnership with a community organization. They generally use the same skills and make the same assumptions that work well for them in forming business partnerships. They engage in defining a win-win-win goal—something that will serve the community, the community partner and the servant-institution. Then they define the roles of each partner and work to fill their own role as effectively as possible.

The servant-institution has many different assets to invest in a community partnership: (1) the time and energy of employees, (2) the participation of customers, (3) the unique skills and resources of the servant-institution, and (4) financial support. Often the servant-institution does what SBLI USA does—it establishes programs and policies to support their employees in pursuit of community involvement. This is most often matching time and/or money that the employee gives to the charity or civic activity of their choice. This multiplies the listening power of the servant-institution. Instead of listening as a function of the organization it is listening as a function of every employee. The result is a positive influence on many more projects and issues than the company could do by itself.

The time and energy leaders invest in community partnerships is powerful. They provide a model of serving the community to other employees. They help shape the image of the company in the community by their personal actions. Jack Lowe, Jr. of TDIndustries serves as board chair of the Dallas Public Schools. In so doing he makes a strong statement to his employees.

Some servant-institutions also find ways to engage their customers in serving the community. Retailers invite their customers to contribute to charities through collection points in their stores. Or they participate in profit sharing programs with their customers such as giving a percent of all sales receipts for a specific time period to one or more charities. Remember the Upromise program of Festival Foods that invests a percentage of money spent by a specific customer into a college savings program for the child of the customer. This program links a group of food producers with a group of grocery stores with a group of families with a community issue—promotion of higher education.

In other cases the investment of a servant-institution is through application of the unique skills and resources of the company. An engineering firm can supply engineers to a Third World clean water project. Or a large company can loan an executive to a United Way agency for a period of time in a critically important point in the growth of the agency. Or a construction firm like TDIndustries can provide tools or equipment for volunteers to use in building homes for families in need.

Finally, investment in the community can take the form of financial support through corporate giving, employee giving, or grants from foundations related historically to the corporation. Investment in the community almost always involves a combination of financial, human and other resources. Any community fundraiser will tell you that organizations don't give—people give.

We have seen two excellent examples of productive community partnerships by two very different servant-institutions: First Fruits and SBLI USA. First Fruits found it natural to want to share their experience with communities in Latin America, Africa and Asia torn apart by sending their men off to be migrant workers far from home. Through a family foundation they created for this purpose, First Fruits has joined with community partners in a half-dozen different countries to address this unique set of issues. And they have done it with all their heart and soul, plus 75 percent of their profits! Their service to the community is focused. They bring to each partner relevant experience, yet they come with great humility. They listen, they learn, they teach, and they build. They are the kind of partners that make a significant difference in the lives of families around the world. They do it because they want to, because they can, and because they believe they are called to do so.

SBLI USA was started over 70 years ago to provide working families in New York City with affordable life insurance through their neighborhood banks. The community SBLI USA chooses to serve beyond their customers is the community of their customers. That community is defined as underserved working families, single parent families, and Hispanic families. SBLI USA brings their expertise in making this community feel empowered to participate in the things that generally are not offered to families of these diverse communities. They have helped to support over 50 different local and national charitable organizations on a wide variety of programs that help the community grow and succeed.

SBLI USA employees are recruited from the community, so it is the SBLI USA employee who drives their community service. Employees choose the organizations and projects they feel are most effective in addressing issues close to them and the causes they believe in most. The company communicates to all of its employees the importance of the particular event or project and urges everyone to get involved. SBLI USA gets totally involved, putting their reputation on the line alongside their customers, employees, and community partners.

One of the common threads of these two examples is that there is little sense of charity—a rich organization giving to the poor. Instead there is a strong sense of service—a servant-institution fully participating in the community of which they are a part.

Led by servant-leaders

In his essay *The Institution as Servant,* Robert K. Greenleaf wrote a great deal about the critical role of trustees. His standard for trustees was:

> ... [C]are for the institution, which means care for all of the people the institution touches
>
> ... [A]ccept the obligation to design and oversee a top administration that is capable of making the impossible possible, i.e., move the institution toward distinction and deal with all of the pressures of these times(24)

Greenleaf was responding to the 1960s crisis in confidence and trust of American institutions when he published this essay in 1972. He included institutions of business, higher education and faith in his sweeping call for reform. How much more urgent Greenleaf might have felt today had he lived to experience the current state of affairs.

What Greenleaf asked of trustees should be asked of boards of directors, of entrepreneurs and venture capitalists, and of heads of family businesses. Someone must play the trustee role in every organization. Someone has to take responsibility for caring for the institution—not just the administration but the institution itself. Someone needs to feel obligated to move the institution toward distinction as servant, and to designing and overseeing the top administration, to make sure that those top leaders are capable of making the impossible possible, while dealing with all of the pressures of these times and future times.

When we look at each of our examples of servant-institutions we see without exception that trustee role being played out by one or more top leaders. Dick Pieper at PPC Partners, Jack Lowe, Jr. at TDIndustries, Ralph Stayer at Johnsonville Sausage, Tom Ogorchock at DuBrook Concrete, Vikki Pryor at SBLI USA Mutual Life Insurance, Dave Skogen at Festival Foods, and Cheryl and Ralph Broetje at First Fruits have all accepted Greenleaf's challenge at their companies, as Ken Melrose did as president and CEO of Toro.

Each experienced his or her own personal transformation at some point from, the power model to the servant model. Each has taken responsibility for seeing that his or her company tries every day to serve its employees, customers, business partners, and community partners. Each makes sure that the long-term picture and core values of trust and respect are at the fore as strategic decisions are made. They are servant-leaders on a journey with their companies, each of which is a unique servant-institution.

Greenleaf calls these top leaders to dream. He said:

> For anything to happen there must be a dream. And for anything great to happen there must be a great dream. One of these great dreams is for the good society made up of predominantly serving institutions that shape its character by encouraging serving individuals and providing scope and shelter for large creative acts of service—by individuals and groups.(25)

Greenleaf also said that foresight is the central ethic of leadership, the "lead" that a leader has. Foresight is the act of anticipating what is likely to happen, generally outside of the control of the organization, that will impact the organization. This includes events and forces that could either have a negative or positive impact. The strongest leaders are those who focus on turning any outside event or force into an opportunity for their organization. They look ahead far enough to have time to figure out what their options are. They fill the time between anticipation and occurrence with creative, strategic planning. They are rarely caught completely off guard.

The Toro Company was on the ropes when Ken Melrose had the foresight to look around at the competition, and saw that it was Honda, a company that planned in terms of decades, not quarters. He had the foresight to see that the challenge was long-term, and that to succeed, Toro would have to plant seed, not sod.

As the leaders of servant-institutions look ahead, over the fence, or around the next corner, they do so through the lens of their commitment to serving everyone touched by the organization, their relationships. As they make plans they repeatedly ask "How will this decision influence the trust we've been building with each of the groups of people affected by this decision?" Greenleaf was certain that "Trust must come first. Nothing will move until trust is firm."(26)

Greenleaf challenged us to make fundamental, radical shifts in how we understand the role of trustees and leaders and managers, and the task of serving employees, customers, business partners and community partners. But Greenleaf would not answer the questions: What is this servant-institution like? What does it take to create one? Instead he said that these questions will have to be answered by those who hold the institution in trust. The eight companies described in this book provide some practical answers in the experiences of their servant-leaders who are working to make their organizations servant-institutions. We encourage you, now, to take advantage of their insights and build your own servant-institution.

Postscript: The Bottom Line

Throughout this book we have assumed that servant-institutions do well in terms of the financial bottom line—return on investment; strong balance sheets; meeting budgets, projections and goals. But we have not focused on the relationship between servant leadership and the bottom line, in part because many of the companies we've described are family businesses, closely held companies or employee owned. We have chosen not to pry into their confidential financials. Thus we have not tried to prove that servant-institutions automatically do well financially.

However, our friends James Sipe and Don Frick have included a very interesting analysis of the financial performance of selected servant-led companies in their new book, *Seven Pillars of Servant Leadership: Practicing the Wisdom of Leading by Serving* (Paulist Press, 2009).

Sipe and Frick, along with their former associate Jeff Pauley of Magellan Executive Resources, compared the companies made famous by Jim Collins's book, *Good to Great*, with companies that have been applying servant leadership principles.

The research was based on the metrics Collins used to evaluate the financial performance of his eleven publicly traded "good to great" companies (Fannie Mae, Circuit City, Nucor, Kroger, Walgreens, Wells Fargo, Altria Group, Gillette, Pitney Bowes, Kimberly Clark, Abbott Laboratories). Those companies were compared with eleven publicly-traded companies that are frequently cited in the literature as being servant-led—Toro Company, Southwest Airlines, Starbucks, AFLAC, Men's Wearhouse, Synovus Financial, Herman Miller, ServiceMasters, Marriott International, FedEx, and Medtronic.

The comparison focused on the ten-year period ending in 2005. The authors found that during those years, stocks from the five hundred largest public companies (i.e., Standard & Poors 500) averaged a 10.8 percent pre-tax portfolio return. The eleven companies studied by Collins averaged a 17.5 percent return. However, the servant-led companies' returns averaged 24.2 percent.

"The bottom line is that the servant-led companies produced far superior financial results," said Sipe, "which led us to a startling conclusion: "servant-led companies are even *better than great!*" (27)

Not all servant-institutions will have better financial returns than their peers. However, this comparison suggests that being a servant-institution does not hurt the bottom line.

All of the people we talked to at servant-institutions reported that in their experience: a) employees who feel served by the organization do a great job of serving customers, b) customers who feel respected by the company and who trust the company buy more from that company, c) business partners who feel they are in win-win-win relationships do the best job they can to reach shared goals, and d) community partners who feel supported by a company welcome that company in the community and tend to support it.

It appears that the important bottom line is how well a business serves all of the people it touches. When the servant bottom line is consistently strong, chances are good the financial bottom line will follow.

Questions For Reflection and Discussion

Serving Employees

1. How does my organization help each employee develop?
2. How does my organization unleash the energy and intelligence of employees?
3. How does my organization train, measure and coach employees in their knowledge, skills and practice of servant leadership?
4. What makes my organization one for which employees feel uniquely proud to work?

Serving Customers

5. How does my organization listen to customers?
6. How does my organization treat customers with respect?
7. How does my organization develop products and services that serve customer needs?

Serving Business Partners

8. How does my organization listen to business partners?
9. How does my organization treat business partners with respect?
10. How does my organization develop productive business relationships with our business partners?

Serving Community Partners

11. How does my organization listen to community partners?
12. How does my organization treat community partners with respect?
13. How does my organization invest in community partnerships?
14. How does my organization develop productive community partnerships?

Led by Servant-Leaders

15. How does my top leadership fulfill the trustee role of caring for the institution and all of the people it touches?
16. How do my top leaders demonstrate their servant-leader skills?
17. How does my top leadership team demonstrate foresight?

Uniqueness

18. How is my organization unique as a servant-institution?
19. How have we moved servant leadership beyond a program or project or event to make it an integrated part of everything about the organization?

Notes

(1) Robert K. Greenleaf, *The Institution as Servant* (Westfield, IN, Greenleaf Center for Servant Leadership, 1972/2009), 9.

(2) Partnership of the Spirit: Culture Video, produced by TDIndustries, Dallas, TX, 2008

(3) www.DuBrookConcrete.com/Employees

(4) www.DuBrookConcrete.com/AboutUs.ServantLeadership

(5) www.DuBrookConcrete.com/Employees

(6) www.DuBrookConcrete.com/Customers

(7) www.DuBrookConcrete.com/Suppliers

(8) www.FirstFruits.com/AboutUS

(9) www.vista-hermosa.org

(10) Id.

(11) www.SBLIUSA.com

(12) www.FestivalFoods.com

(13) www.johnsonville.com

(14) www.jobs.johnsonville.com/home/culture/values

(15) Id.

(16) Ken Melrose, *Making the Grass Greener on Your Side* (San Francisco: Berrett-Koehler, 1996), 53-69.

(17) Id. 27.

(18) Id. 11.

(19) Id. 74-76.

(20) Id. 17-18.

(21) Tom Bamberger, *Stories from the Field* (Milwaukee: PPC Partners, 2008), 77.

(22) Id.

(23) Howard Behar, *It's Not About the Coffee* (New York: Portfolio, 2007), 49.

(24) Robert K. Greenleaf, *The Institution as Servant,* 15, 31.

(25) Id. 49.

(26) Id.

(27) James W. Sipe & Don M. Frick, *Seven Pillars of Servant Leadership: Practicing the Wisdom of Leading by Serving* (Mahwah, NJ: Paulist Press, 2009), 2.

Acknowledgments

Writing this book was only possible because of the great work being done by all of the good people at the eight companies discussed—collectively thousands of women and men. I would like to especially thank individuals at each company who helped by letting me talk with them often and by reading and reacting to drafts of this book: Jack Lowe, Jr., at TDIndustries, Colin Searcy at DuBrook, Vikki Pryor at SBLI USA, Dave Skogen at Festival Foods, Cory Bouck at Johnsonville Sausage, Ken Melrose at Toro, and Dick Pieper at PPC Partners.

I would like to thank Kent Keith for his guiding style of coaching and for sharing his rich experience with both servant leadership and publishing. He led me through the process of writing this book using all seven key practices of a servant-leader.

Thanks also to Heidi Newman for her expert copyediting. I wish I'd had her help several projects ago!

About the Author

Jerry Glashagel is Program Consultant at the Greenleaf Center for Servant Leadership. He has been involved in program development and training with YMCAs and other non-profits for almost five decades. He has also had a parallel, entrepreneurial career with ventures in housing, international trade and community banking.

Mr. Glashagel earned degrees in sociology (University of Illinois) and theology (Yale Divinity School). His current focus is on listening—both for the benefit of the listener and speaker. He is a member of the international Motivational Interviewing Training Network. His favorite people to listen to include his wife of over 40 years, their two children and four grandchildren.

Mr. Glashagel is a consultant with Triangle2 LLC, and can be reached at jglashagel@greenleaf.org or jglashagel@triangle2.com.

About the Greenleaf Center

The Greenleaf Center for Servant Leadership was founded in 1964 by Robert Greenleaf as the Center for Applied Ethics. It was renamed for him in 1985. The Center is an international non-profit organization dedicated to promoting the understanding and practice of servant leadership.

The Center's website, www.greenleaf.org, provides information and resources on servant leadership. The Center's Annual International Conference on Servant Leadership attracts learners and practitioners from around the world. Over the years, keynote speakers have included James Autry, Ken Blanchard, Peter Block, Stephen Covey, Max DePree, Joseph Jaworski, James Kouzes, Peter Senge, and Margaret Wheatley. The Center's Speakers Bureau provides keynote speakers for conferences. The Center also offers Greenleaf Seminars for organizations wishing to introduce or reinforce key concepts and practices of servant-leaders and of servant-institutions to their leadership teams. The Center's programs include the annual Leadership Institute for Education (LIFE), which offers information and encouragement to educational leaders who wish to practice servant leadership in their institutions.

To become a member or donor, or to learn more about our services, please contact us at:

The Greenleaf Center for Servant Leadership
770 Pawtucket Drive
Westfield, IN 46074

Tel. 317-669-8050
Fax 317-669-8055
www.greenleaf.org